BRIGHT BOOTS

BRIGHT BOOTS

AN AUTOBIOGRAPHY

FRED GRESSWELL

David & Charles
Newton Abbot London North Pomfret (Vt)

To my mother,
to whom I owe my bright boots,
and
to my wife and family,
who have made them easy wearing

British Library Cataloguing in Publication Data

Gresswell, Fred
Bright boots.—2nd ed.
1. Gresswell, Fred 2. Real estate agents
—Great Britain—Biography
I. Title
333.33′0924 HD298

ISBN 0-7153-8400-7

First published by Robert Hale Ltd in 1956

Typeset by ABM Tyopgraphics Limited, Hull
and printed in Great Britain
by Redwood Burn Limited Trowbridge, Wilts
for David & Charles (Publishers) Limited
Brunel House Newton Abbot Devon

Published in the United States of America
by David & Charles Inc
North Pomfret Vermont 05053 USA

CONTENTS

I should not talk so much about myself, if there was anyone else I knew so well. Unfortunately I am confined to this theme by the narrowness of my experience. Moreover, I on my side, require of every writer, first or last, a simple and small account of his own life, not merely what he has heard of other men's lives, some such account as he would send to his kindred from a distant land. Perhaps these pages are more particularly addressed to poor students; as for the rest of my readers they will accept such portions as apply to them.

Thoreau, *Walden*

INTRODUCTION

Success stories, written by so-called captains of industry, were popular reading when I was a young man, the theme being 'How To Get On In The World'. Nobody wanted to know the secret more than I. Making money and getting rich was, I thought, the criterion of success, and the recipe usually prescribed was honesty, hard work and thrift. However, I had exploited these virtues to the full before I was ten years of age, and discovered they had not got me very far!

Later, when I came into personal contact with self-made men, I found that, while these principles were useful as a foundation, it was the indefinable *plus* that made the real difference. I learnt, for example, that the men who 'made good' financially were generally more astute than their fellows and unafraid to take chances when occasion demanded. They had, of course, to work for themselves, not for an employer.

Times have changed greatly since I was young. The incident of taxation has made great wealth more difficult to accumulate and less easy to retain. Nowadays, most would-be millionaires must be prepared to dedicate their lives to the cause of business. In addition to overcoming normal commercial hazards, they must be prepared to hand over a large percentage of the rewards of their efforts to the National Exchequer, and even if the occasional genius succeeds for a time in outwitting the tax-gatherers, he will find himself in the end trapped by the same man in a different guise on his death bed.

For readers who may come across this book several years hence, I should perhaps point out that the pence and shillings mentioned in the earlier chapters of the book changed after decimalisation was introduced into Britain. To illustrate, here are some equivalences:

Before decimalisation	*After decimalisation*
6d (sixpence)	2½p (pence)
1s (shilling, used to be 12 old pence)	5p
10s	50p

I ought perhaps to explain how my personal story came to be written. Like most people I had many secret desires and ambitions, but writing an autobiography was not one of them. What I wanted to do was to publish an anthology, and for a simple reason. Up to the age of twenty I had not read a worthwhile book; I had received a very elementary education and my mind was mediocre. Then it was my good fortune to come under the influence of men and books that profoundly altered the course of my life and gave to it an unusual slant. I began to collect quotations from books and other sources from which I gradually developed my own attitude to life, making at this point a thorough analysis of myself. I examined my strengths and my weaknesses as honestly and objectively as I could. The result enabled me to compromise with material fortune and achieve a large measure of happiness.

When I first thought of writing the book, a publisher told me he was interested in my story but not in an anthology, so only a few of my collection of quotations were added at the end of the first edition, which was published in 1956. This new and updated edition omits the quotations and is published in my ninety-first year.

My wife asked me not to mention her or her family business in the original book, and I have often been reproved for not having done so. Now, as a tribute to her memory – which I know will give as much satisfaction to her friends as it does to me – I include her story. I believe it is more interesting than mine, and in any event it will undoubtedly show how much she was responsible for my early success. I have also recorded other important incidents which were not included in the first edition.

Finally, let me explain the title of the book. When I asked my mother what had been her guiding ambition, she replied immediately: 'I always told your father I never cared how many children we had if I could be sure they all wore bright boots'. Nobody who has even an inkling of the nature of the hard work on a small-holding will need an explanation of that phrase.

I

MY PEOPLE

> The villager born humbly and bred hard
> Content his wealth and poverty his guard,
> His means but scanty and his wants but few,
> Labour his business and his pleasure too.
>
> CHURCHILL

I was born in the village of Digby, in Lincolnshire, in the early 'nineties. I saw little of the gaiety usually associated with that decade. From the age of seven to the age of thirteen I certainly worked harder and longer than I have ever done since. This is not a complaint. It did me no harm, and I have since appreciated leisure more than most people.

As the story of my early years is linked with the village, I would like to say something about it and its inhabitants.

The history of Digby goes back at least 1,000 years. It is mentioned in the Domesday record. To this day it is a wholly rural area, and few of us were far above the peasantry, proud or otherwise.

The following is an extract from *Sketches of New and Old Sleaford,* 1825.

> *Digby.* This village is very retired, rural and pleasant, with a small rivulet of beautiful water running through part of it. There is a stone cross, in a high state of preservation, standing a short distance south-east of the Church, which being the only perfect one in this part of the country, is consequently an object of much interest. The enclosure of the parish took place in the year 1720.

It further states:

In noticing the population of this parish, the reader doubtless will be struck, as we ourselves were, with a very singular circumstance in the two parliamentary returns which we transcribe. The one, in 1801, returns Digby as having fifty-four inhabited houses, fifty-seven families, and a population of two hundred and forty-two persons, and also two houses untenanted. The other, twenty years subsequent, viz. 1821, states this place to have but fifty houses in the whole, and all inhabited; but what appears very remarkable is, that although the number of inhabited houses is reduced by four, the number of families is increased by seven, viz. to sixty-four, making a population of two hundred and seventy-seven persons. There were in Queen Elizabeth's days fifty-three families here.

The population in 1901 was 351, a figure which shows very little variation over the centuries.

The only houses that appear to have been built in the nineteenth century were six cottages which were let at 1s 6d a week. There were certainly no new buildings erected during the 'nineties. The only change I remember in the district during these years was made by a progressive householder in the next village of Dorrington, who had a bow window built out from his cottage. This was such a novelty that people would walk over from other villages to see it, and farmers passing on their way to market would rein in their horses to admire it.

There were three farms of from 200 to 400 acres each in Digby, and several small holdings. Farmers came and went, but three families constituted the backbone of the village community. There were the Baumbers, the Sumners and the Browns. We were a branch of the Sumner family, a cut above the labouring class, but not up to the tradesman standard. My maternal grandfather was one of a family of ten, and himself, born in the year of Waterloo, brought up a family of eleven. He was a man of striking, even artistocratic appearance, and indeed he had come from a good family which we understood had been brought down in the world through drink. He was the youngest of the ten children, and his share in the family estate was 20 acres of land, two horses and wagons.

As there was no railway at that time in Digby, he used to take these horses and wagons to Lincoln, fourteen miles away. There they were filled up with coal, which was then retailed in the village by the bucket. My mother told me that, when her father was doing odd jobs in the village, she often went with her mother to Lincoln to fetch the coal. They had to walk the fourteen miles home again behind the laden wagons.

At that time grandfather was one of the few people in the village who could write. In consequence, he was in constant demand as a scribe for the farm servants. He told me that on one occasion a labourer came and asked him to compose a letter to his sweetheart, who lived fourteen miles away. The young man was so pleased with it that he said: 'By goy, boy, that's good! I'll tak' it missen.' And he did.

Grandfather lived to be eighty-five; grandmother died two years before him, aged eighty-three, on the day Mafeking was relieved. I was then about ten, and I always remember going back with my grandfather to his cottage after the funeral. When we entered, he walked across to the mantelpiece, took down his pipe, filled it, lit it and sat down in his highbacked chair with this unadorned remark: 'Well, she has been a good wife to me.' Although I was still very young, this seemed to me to bring death down to a more understandable level.

The living standards just before my time were those of near-poverty. My grandmother's allowance for groceries was 2s 6d a week. To keep the doctor, an expensive luxury, away, she acquired a knowledge of herbal remedies. She weighed her butter on home-made scales of wood, the counter-balancing weight being 1lb of sugar from the grocer's. The education of that generation was no more than a smattering. Children were fed largely on bread and lard, skimmed milk and vegetables. They were destined, if boys, for hard work on the land; if girls, for domestic service. Even so, social status within this rural circle was acutely defined, and perhaps the case of my father and mother can be taken as typical.

My mother's people were well up in the village social scale. Their family of twelve was equally divided between sons and daughters. The sons were mainly connected with machinery, and two of them were in partnership, owning traction engines for threshing corn and sawing wood. At that time the fens were being reclaimed, and another of the boys was in charge of the pumping station. The daughters, one of whom was my mother, were in better-class domestic service, and most of them got married just above the working-class level to men in some sort of trade. The outstanding case was that of the youngest, Aunt Emma, the good-looking one of the family, who brought off the biggest triumph by marrying an innkeeper.

Mother herself was moving upwards through the domestic service channels from a small farmhouse to a larger, then to a vicarage, and then to the Hall at Ashby-de-la-Launde. At nineteen she was earning £20 a year, when she threw all her excellent prospects to the winds and married my father – a farm labourer who came from the bread-and-seam class, seam being the local word for lard.

By the way, it was at Ashby Hall that a great figure of the First World War started to climb the ladder of fame. This was Field Marshall Sir William Robertson, who just before my mother's time began his active career as a humble hall-boy in that great house.

A townsman would see no difference between one farm labourer and another, but to a countryman there were distinct gradations. There were the yeoman type, who in addition to working for others, might rent a few acres of land for themselves. These were usually church people, and because of this received some slight education. Until the middle of the nineteenth century the only chance the village people had of acquiring any learning appears to have been through religious channels.

The other type were the genuine clodhoppers. They usually had large families, and too often the men drank away the vital 1s or 2s a week. The women might be shiftless. They were usually dull mentally and slow in movement, inarticulate and entirely illiterate. They might be good workers, but they were doomed to be labourers, and unless they were lucky they could finish in the workhouse.

I don't know anything about my father's parents. I never heard him speak of them, except to say his father was a shepherd, and lived on an isolated farm on the heath near the hamlet of Braunce-well. This is situated about 2 miles from what is now Cranwell Aerodrome.

In those days it made a big difference where people lived. If it was near the church, the parson or the squire saw to it that they attended, but shepherds were excused, having their flocks to look after, and my father's people belonged to that group.

Father started going into the fields with his father as soon as he could walk. With sheep there were odd jobs the smallest boy could do. At six years of age he started to work regularly, minding horses, tending cows, picking stones, scaring crows, etc. His food consisted of bread and lard and sometimes bread and onions, with hot vegetables and skimmed milk at night. He was lucky to taste meat once a week on a Sunday. At the age of ten he was going out with the horses and having meals on the farm, only sleeping at home. In spite of such a rough upbringing he was physically strong, and developed into a powerfully built young man.

My parents started married life with a capital of £5. My father's wage as an agricultural labourer was then 15s a week, without cottage or other extras, but this fell to an average of 12s in winter through time lost during bad weather.

My mother's instincts were right. She had chosen the man most suited to her dynamic personality. She married beneath her. She stooped to conquer. Though the couple were not ostracised by her family, there was a tacit agreement that they would keep themselves to themselves. In any case, to be married with only £5 for everything in the way of furnishing did not provide much to entertain with – but it was not so much the money that divided them. Her sisters might have married on £25; the difference was all in social status. People with cloths on the table did not mix with people who ate off oilcloth or even newspaper. It took about fifteen years for mother to stage a spectacular comeback.

Both mother and father had superabundant health and neither of them knew their own strength, but it was mother who directed their efforts towards acquiring capital. In the normal way, however hard a labourer worked, and however careful and thrifty his wife might be, it could take a lifetime to acquire a house sufficiently equipped with furniture to receive their grown-up children. Mother was tall and lean, full of restless energy, with a strong will and an indomitable spirit; a great worker and fighter. She used to think nothing of working eighteen hours a day, starting at six in the morning, and never spared herself or anyone else within her reach. Father had no idea of business, and it was always a source of wonder to him that he had been able to marry someone who could start a banking account and build up some small resources. He had only one comment: 'I don't know how you've done it!'

Within his limitations he certainly fulfilled his part. He had no vices or extravagances except that of smoking ½oz of shag a week, and this would be suspended in cases of emergency. He was a quiet, unassuming man with a fund of natural wisdom. When they eventually obtained a very small holding he was in his element. He could then work nearly night and day. He would clean out the cowshed, get the pig food ready and other jobs done before walking two miles to work, where he was due at 6am. When he came home at night in summer he was off to the allotment spreading muck, making hay, attending to stock and innumerable jobs. There was no Saturday afternoon off. He laboured all the hours of daylight and, even on winter nights, he took down the stable lanterns immediately after tea and worked until bedtime. In those days I don't think he was ever tired. I never heard him say so.

On Sundays he did not work on the land, but he was fully occupied all day. He did the milking and looking after the stock in the early morning, then walked 2 miles to Ashby Church where he was a bell-ringer for morning service; in the afternoon and evening he attended service at Digby Chapel, as I shall describe. After chapel on Sunday evening was his only hour of recreation. This he spent learning to read. The Sunday-school provided cards showing the alphabet in capital and small letters. These he memorised when working during the week, and later my sister stood on a stool at the back of his chair and told him how to spell the words. Reading became his main recreation eventually. Father was the complete all-round farm man. Most men excelled in some special job, especially if there was a chance of piece-work, but he was an expert sheep-shearer, thatcher (called 'thacker'), hedger and ditcher.

In her early married life mother went to work at farmhouses, and took child-bearing in her stride. One of her jobs was milking twelve cows twice a day, including Sundays, for 6d a week each.

Eventually they saved up enough to buy an extra pig for breeding. When the first litter was sold they had accumulated £10. With this capital they were able to rent a cottage with a 2½-acre paddock, and out of this they started to achieve their independence. First they bought a cow and gradually over a period of years built up a small herd of five or six cattle, also a stock of hens and pigs. For several years there was no thought of buying anything for the house. Everything was ploughed into stock of some sort. Our holding consisted of two tumbledown cottages with a good garden, a shed for three cows, and other outbuildings. The land was good and the garden would grow anything.

Mother took the young children with her when she went out to work until they were old enough to look after one another. At the age of seven they went out to work with only two or three days a week at school. Children were paid 4d a day for pulling ketlocks (large weeds growing among the corn), setting and picking potatoes, singling mangolds, etc. In winter they worked all the hours of daylight, and my sister said they often came home from work by moonlight. Except on Sundays when mother cooked a dinner, the meals were very much catch-as-catch-can. The only meat we had was bacon, which was always served hot with vegetables for the evening meal. Father took a quarter of a loaf of bread and a chunk of cold fat bacon. These he sliced with a jack knife for his nine o'clock breakfast and one o'clock dinner, which he ate in the fields. It was rarely that he carried any other food with him, though on odd occasions he might have the remnants of a fruit pie. At home we always had a boiling of cold bacon on the table for breakfast and lunch. The only extra we had in a morning as a very special treat was toast and fried potatoes and at our midday meal we sometimes had a milk pudding.

Further progress was made by obtaining the tenancy of the 2-acre vicarage field at Ashby. This was poor land and two miles from home, but it served a useful purpose for many years. In due course my parents wanted to improve the cottage and buildings in Digby. Mother decided that the only thing to do was to buy the property. After much negotiation it passed to us for £200. A tremendous effort was made to find the deposit, and the balance was obtained on mortgage from the local Sick Club. Evidently this loan was a humiliation to my mother. One day I told her that a boy at school had revealed to me that we had a 'monkey' (slang word for mortgage) on our house. She immediately went to the solicitor and had the mortgage transferred to the local Co-operative Society.

Father was now for consolidating. The height of his ambition was 3 acres and a cow, but the children were growing up and mother formed a resolution that was to be the basis of her life's work. Her children were to be better off than she had ever been, to wear 'bright boots', and from then on her life was dedicated to that end.

I was the fifth child and born about this period. By the time I was ready for work at seven there were plenty of tasks at home, and I was saved the humiliating experience of going out to work. The only job I did outside was a few days' crow scaring at my own request. There was never a waking moment without half a dozen jobs waiting. The field at Ashby was our meadow field but did not provide the fodder required, and what are known as 'accommodation fields' were hard to get. A field is something and nothing on a large farm, but to a small-holder it can mean the breath of life.

The parish had acquired 10 acres, which were divided into allotments of roods for people with large families and small-holders, and my parents were renting more than their share for growing roots for the cattle. It was there I learnt what a back-aching job land work was and I determined I would try and find some other way of earning a living.

Mother's only solution was hard work. She never compromised

or tried to find an easy way out. She was ruthless in demanding a full quota of work from every member of the family and equally scathing in her condemnation of lazy and thriftless people. A field of 6 acres of good land next to the allotment came on the market. It was the only single field I remember being sold at Digby. The price was £300. Mother was desperate to get it since it would absorb all the stock capacity of our holding. Somehow the necessary deposit was found. This meant another fierce struggle to earn halfpennies, pennies and shillings. We never thought in terms of pounds – only mother knew where they went. It was not until this hurdle was taken that mother could turn her attention to our social amenities.

It was at this time that the almost derelict cottage adjoining ours became vacant, and it was decided, much against father's inclinations, to build a new wing on our house. A jobbing builder we knew got the contract. The price was £90. It was a very low estimate; the builder was a hard worker and willing, but weak and rather inefficient. His name was Clay, but he was certainly putty in mother's hands. We got our full money's worth.

The only thing that escaped mother's eagle eye was the quality of plaster that went into the ceiling. This nearly had fatal results soon after it was finished. She gave birth to my youngest brother, and on the following day the ceiling of the bedroom came down. They would have been buried but for the canopy on the four-poster bed. Now that we had a sitting-room and two extra bedrooms, however, they had to be furnished, complete with a harmonium, which put the coping stone on the newly built social fabric.

The family assets now being in the region of £200, there was nothing to prevent the resumption of relations with mother's family on equal terms. Full family status was restored when father appeared in frock coat and top hat at Aunt Emma's wedding to mine host of the Black Bull, Sleaford. Visits were now regularly exchanged, and on the first of these Aunt Emma gave me 4d. Mother had won her long battle.

In the town of Sleaford, seven miles from Digby, there was published annually *Morton's Lincolnshire Almanack,* price 2d, which was taken by nearly every household in the district. It contained not only a full description of the villages, but the names of all the heads of the households, from the squire down to the farm labourers. In the case of the latter, however, only the names were stated, and until I was ten my father appeared as 'Gresswell, L.'. I remember the thrill when I read for the first time, 'Gresswell, L., Cottager and Parish Councillor'. The term 'cottager' denoted the possession of a small-holding. My father had reached the age of forty before he achieved this eminence.

It was a characteristic of mother that having reached a certain standard of living she must now start improving and beautifying our home. All we had had before was one wild rose tree that twined round the pump outside the kitchen door and gave the place the name of Rose Cottage. Now she planted a flower garden, a rarity in Digby, at the front of the house – roses, stocks, asters, mignonette and the rest. In due course she set out an orchard of excellent fruit trees, interspersed with such decorative things as weeping willow and drooping ash.

We soon found that our extra accommodation carried responsibilities as well as privileges. Grandmother died about this time, and grandfather had to find somewhere else to go, so mother decided that it was her duty to look after him. He had no money, and although efforts were made to get the family to contribute towards his keep, apparently none of them could be compelled to do so; they all had more than two children and only small incomes. He had to accept parish relief, which was 3s 6d per week, supplemented by my Aunt Emma, who made a contribution of 1s 6d a week. While mother accepted this burden, she did not forget to let the other members of the family know that she thought they were evading their responsibilities. Grandfather brought with him his chair, bed and other bits and pieces of furniture; also his desk, which was much coveted by the family. This desk had an air of mystery about it, and occupied the place of honour in our living-room. Grandfather sometimes showed me several secret drawers in which, in my imagination, I thought he hoarded golden sovereigns, but he always kept it locked.

His coming to our house involved changes in the domestic

arrangements and more regular mealtimes. He had a hearty appetite, and was accustomed to home comforts and three regular meals a day. He certainly ate us out of house and home for the next two years.

When he died, even before the funeral, there were rumblings which preceded the storm of family clashes. These were kept in check until after the funeral, when the eldest son demanded the desk. However mother was prepared for this, and apparently she had the right to sell his odds and ends to pay for the funeral expenses. Whether we claimed the desk as part of these I don't know, but in spite of many efforts, and almost stand-up fights, it remained in my parents' possession. I was very excited when for the first time we looked inside the desk to find out what was in the secret drawers. Unfortunately, they contained only nails, screws and suchlike.

After grandfather's death we began to enjoy the comfort of the extra accommodation. The family fortunes also improved in respect of income and prestige. Mother became a postal official, and I started in business for myself.

The post came by road carrier, which served the high road from Lincoln to Sleaford. It was an imposing vehicle, and the driver sat on a large red box on which was painted in gold letters 'ROYAL MAIL'. Very often the mail was late, and I was then sent to the top road to keep a look-out. This saved mother waiting at the post office, a small house in the centre of the village, and the business was transacted in the kitchen scullery. The route mother covered delivering letters was officially measured as three miles out and two miles in, and the time allowed for walking was from 7.30 to 11.30am, for which the pay was 7s weekly, with uniform. She used to sell stamps on the round, and we liked to describe her as the 'Rowston postmistress' although the official designation was 'postwoman'. But this was a considerable promotion from the status of washerwoman and constituted a definite rise in the social scale.

Mother soon found that valuable time could be saved by cycling instead of walking, so she saved the money she earned and invested in a pneumatic-tyred bicycle. She expected to be able to ride it straightaway, and as she had not much patience she had many spills. It irked her to see other people being able to sit straight and control their machines, and she got really annoyed and blamed the bicycle. Father had to teach her to ride, and was the one who suffered most. He did more running then than he did for the rest of his life.

The improvement in our social status had some comic consequences. I had heard of children's parties but had never been to one. When the new sitting-room was ready I asked mother if I could have a party on Christmas Day. At first she refused, and then compromised by giving me permission to ask a friend to tea. Most of the boys that I knew were having their own family parties, but the boy who accepted the invitation was the only one in a large family of girls, and I suppose he thought it would be a change.

I knew John was a very quiet boy, but thought it was shyness, and I was looking forward to bringing him out. He came early. Mother had given us the use of the sitting-room, but this entertaining business was new to both of us, and we could not find anything to say. The only game we had was Ludo, which I was reserving for after tea, and it was a great relief to me when it was time to eat. John certainly did justice to the meal, during which he never uttered a word but took everything that was offered. If he was addressed at all he would respond with a half-chuckle.

After tea we played Ludo and ate a dessert of apples, nuts and figs. After that there was just nothing to do and, thinking he would be bored, I suggested that as it was dark I would go part of the way home with him. He said no, it was all right, but made no move whatever to go. It was the longest evening as a boy that I ever remember, and I was greatly relieved when father came with a stable lantern and said that he would see him home.

2
EARLY YEARS

A time there was, ere England's griefs began,
  When every rood of ground maintained its man;
For him light labour spread her wholesome store,
  Just gave what life required, but gave no more:
His best companions, innocence and health,
  And his best riches ignorance of wealth.

GOLDSMITH

My mother, who died at 103, always enjoyed life. She once told me that she had achieved most of the things in life she had set out to attain. In her latter years she lived alone in Digby, fully occupied, both mentally and physically, doing her own housework. We are a long-lived family, one of my brothers lived to be ninety-five and my sister lived to be ninety-four.

Father died at the age of eighty-five from pneumonia. He continued to work up to a few days before his death. He was an easy-going man, in stature short and stocky, with a fresh complexion, and slow of speech. He always prefaced an opinion by saying: 'It all depends', and we would then wait, knowing that his mind was working on a problem. It might take him a long time. On one occasion I asked him if he could tell me how much the allotments, which were let off in poles and perches and roods, worked out per acre. It was rather late at night, and I remember having my supper and putting my slippers on, quite forgetting my question. But as I was on the stairs, going to bed, the answer came: 'About £2 an acre, some more and some less, but about £2.'

Only once was he known to give a quick retort. At the end of the First World War the village council were considering some permanent memorial of the victory. My father favoured lighting the street with oil lamps. Another faction wanted to install a clock in the church tower. The leader of the opposition met my father passing the church and asked: 'What time is it Luke?' My father replied: 'Lighting-up time.' But it was more than thirty years later before street lighting won the day. It was installed in the village about 1954.

In those days everything moved at a slow pace, and village news depended either on meetings at market or on gossip from the local carrier, a man with a horse and covered van who used to go round the various country markets every week. He would carry messages or do shopping for people in the village in his particular area.

We were talking to him one night when he told us that Jim Edenbrow had run away from home. This young man, who lived in the next village of Dorrington, a mile and a half away, was looked upon as a steady young man in our district. At twenty-five he was already a local preacher, and this information was disconcerting. Father said: 'And when did you get to know?' The carrier replied: 'Two days ago'. Then father quoted the old adage: 'Ill news travels fast.' To our relief we found out later that Jim had not run away but had merely gone into lodgings to be nearer his work.

Father had a simple faith in the Bible, and in all circumstances he could produce the appropriate text. For instance, he had complete faith in nature doing her part, and however bad the drought or flood, he had one answer: 'Seed time and harvest shall not cease.'

From the age of seven I was fully occupied with many duties that took up all my spare time from school. I do not ever remember playing an organised school game. Certainly we had no football or cricket though, shortly after I left, school clubs were formed to play both games in the village, and later tennis and bowls became popular. We did, however, occasionally play marbles or spin tops. In those days children used to spend their leisure gazing at the sweets in the village shop or listening to the gossip of the grown-ups.

It was also the custom to go two miles to the woods to gather violets at Easter and to spend at least one day blackberrying, which we called brambling, in the autumn. Then there were the adventurous spirits who travelled long distances, mushrooming. Only courting couples went for walks. The only time I went for a walk as a boy was during nature study at school. This bored us all to tears; we knew more than the schoolmaster!

Only once do I remember a circus and menagerie coming to our village in my boyhood. For weeks beforehand the walls and shops were plastered with highly coloured pictures of the delights in store. Every day the school yard was full of children playing lions and tigers, elephants and monkeys. The whole village turned out when the menagerie arrived at last, and of course the star turn for us was the elephant, because of his size. The show was on a Wednesday night, and admission for children was 3d.

At that time we were preparing for a Grand Bazaar at the chapel, and every month there was a coffee supper to raise funds for it. Coffee was quite a luxury in the village, and this was the only occasion on which it was drunk. As it happened, there was a coffee supper, which I attended, the night before the circus. The next night my father was planning his evening in the garden as usual. I said I wanted to go to the menagerie. He said: 'Didn't you go to the coffee supper last night?' I said, 'Yes', and he replied: 'Well you can't go to every dog hanging!' So I did my work in the garden and slipped away at dusk, just before the show opened.

Though I did not have the 3d to go in, it was still the most thrilling experience I had ever had, because it was the first time I had seen moving pictures. Outside the booth, to attract the patrons, the showman had erected a cinematograph, and I saw people on the screen actually walking out of a train and giving up their tickets at the barrier.

I cannot remember myself or any member of the family having any illness except measles. On rare occasions when I imagined I had something wrong I could always eat, and mother said there was nothing wrong with anybody who could eat. (She herself was a hearty eater.) I came home from a party late one night when she was about ninety and she said: 'What about some supper?' I said, 'No, it's a bit late', and she replied: 'I'm having some cold ham and pickles. I've had meat three times a day all my life and always shall.' She was certainly as strong as a horse in her heyday. I myself have seen her put a pitchfork through a rat in mid-air when it flew at her after being cornered in a manger. As far as eating was concerned her motto was, 'Every word hinders a champ', and we were not encouraged to spend time dawdling over food.

Getting wet through did not seem to trouble us either. We had no mackintoshes, and if it rained we wore an overcoat or an old sack. We were often drenched, but mother only commented: 'You're not salt, you won't melt.' Only on one occasion did I feel a sense of grievance.

One bitterly cold day I was working with father in the allotment. We were pulling mangolds out of the ground and chopping the tops off. My knife slipped and I gashed the little finger of my left hand, cutting the nail in two. I could not feel pain. My hands were blue with cold, and I remember saying hopefully to my father: 'I had better go home with this.' He looked at it and said, 'No, I'll tie it up with tar marl. You'll be all right.' I worked with the blood oozing out and the dirt seeping in. I came to no harm, but the nail has never healed up.

On weekdays it did not matter what clothes we wore. We usually had what was handed down to us, but as I was fourth in the line of succession, when the clothes reached me their condition usually left much to be desired. Bearing in mind, no doubt, that there were a further two to clothe after me, my parents bought me one day a new suit of corduroy. This was not the soft flimsy material that nowadays masquerades under the name, but a hard, board-like fabric which could almost stand up by itself when not in use. I shall never forget the rank smell it gave off when new. For the first few days I avoided close contact with other people and talked to them from the opposite side of the room. The one virtue of this corduroy was that it was hard-wearing.

We had our very own Sunday suits, which were renewed every few years on the chapel anniversary. Father rarely wore his best boots except to go to chapel twice on Sundays. As a result he needed only one pair in his long married life.

He used to shave once a week, every Saturday night, which was the time for a general cleaning-up. Every so often heads had to be inspected. It is surprising what village children collect from animals, not to mention from each other. There were no baths in the village, and while I often heard of people who washed their heads and feet, we never knew anyone who washed in between.

There were also no water closets. Every house had an earth closet, called a 'petty'. Some of the larger families had two- and three-holers, situated next to the ash-bin; the mixture in due course manured the garden. It was quite common to use hedges when the petty was full. Unfortunately we kept bees next door to the petty. I was afraid of bees, and towards the end of the season the drones crawled all over the walls and seat. In consequence, I didn't go near the place at this time of the year for weeks on end.

While I was at school, parish water was introduced into the village. Up until then every house had either a well or a pump for drinking water and a tub to catch rainwater for washing. They were distinguished as 'hard' and 'soft' water. The amenity of a cottage was often judged by its water supply. We had a very good well with a pump, but some of the wells used to run dry, and then the cottager would go to the public well. This erection had a roof over it and was a combination of a well and lock-up. The lock-up was an ingenious arrangement. The delinquent sat on a seat opposite the hole of the well so that if he moved he would step straight into the water.

The first indication we had that running water was being installed in the village came when the water diviner arrived. This man walked up and down the street with a hazel twig. It was fascinating to see it turn in his hands. Everybody, of course, had a go, but only one girl had the gift.

In the first place they installed a tap for each of the three thoroughfares, officially named Church Street, Beck Street, and North Street, although the first two were referred to locally as 'Up Street' and 'Down Street'. We were favoured in having one outside our gate but I don't remember using tap water. This supply failed later on, however, and I think eventually water must have been brought in from elsewhere, for today there is a mains supply in most cottages in the village.

3
THE VILLAGE SCHOOL

> A man he was to all the country dear, and passing rich with Forty Pounds a year.
>
> GOLDSMITH

The village school was a church school, with a grant from the education authorities, which varied a good deal according to the standard of results. My eldest brother was apparently one of the first pupils in the early 'eighties. From then on until about my tenth year there seems to have been a succession of schoolmasters, many of whom had very few, if any, qualifications. Some of them were intemperate. In the early days there were about forty scholars of all ages, accommodated in one room. The numbers had risen, when I started, to about seventy, still all in the same room.

The school served most of the immediate districts, except Ashby, and many of the children had to walk two or three miles over fields and rough footpaths. According to Kelly's Directory, the schoolmaster's emoluments in 1889 were £20 16s yearly, with the funds paid out of a charity to the teachers for teaching eight free scholars. This was a remarkable charity in that it was apparently left by a working man. In Archdeacon Trollope's *History of Digby* he writes:

> Henry Young, gardener to the Duke of Rutland, who died in 1761 gave 9 acres of land in Frieston for the benefit of four poor widows of this Parish and a house, each of whom was to have 5s on St. Thomas's Day and the remainder of the proceeds of this land to be applied to the education of eight poor children. There is a tablet in the Church commemorating this humble benefactor.

The charity has several notable features. It was remarkable enough that a native of Digby, obviously from the labouring classes, should have acquired in his lifetime 9 acres of land, and left what must have been a life's savings to the village; also that 9 acres of land has been a safe investment and produced income for 200 years, even if the value of the income had dwindled. Also it is interesting to know that money values did remain stable during the first 150 years, a period during which the charity served a good and useful purpose. Probably the only education that the labouring people got in the village before elementary schools was due to this charity. My own family benefited. The records show that an elder brother obtained a free place, which meant that his fee of 2d a week was paid by the charity.

I recently had the opportunity of inspecting the school log book for the years 1880-1900. This gives some idea of the difficulties experienced during this period.

From HM Inspector's Report for 15 July 1885. 'Since the death of the schoolmaster, the school has been carried on by a youth, who obtained a very unfavourable report as a preparatory teacher in a neighbouring school last year; it has been going downhill as fast as it could. With the exception of reading, the whole work is very unsatisfactory. The master does not know what average attendance means. The managers would do well to obtain at once a capable teacher which the school income can well afford.'

I was interested to find out what type of man this was, and the following entries in his log book are typical of his efforts during the period of his incumbency:

1884	Nov. 17th	Pay particular attention to Standard 3's arithmetic.
	Dec. 2nd	Work as usual.
	Dec. 5th	There has been good attendance during the week. Pay particularly good.
	Dec. 8th	Attendance very good. Pay particular . . .
	Dec. 10th	Pay particular attendance to upper standard's arithmetic.

	Dec. 11th	Work as usual.
1885	Jan. 9th	Pay particular attention to Std. 1 and 2's arithmetic.
	Jan. 12th	Work as usual.
	Jan. 14th	Pay particular attention to Std. 4's arithmetic.
	Mar. 12th	Pay particular attention to upper class arithmetic.
	Mar. 23rd	Good attendance. Pay very good. Learning words of song, 'Twinkle, twinkle, little star'.

It will be noticed that he laid great emphasis on the word 'pay'. This refers to the weekly fee of 2d he got from parents. One entry runs: 'A third child belonging to the family of Gresswell's admitted today and can therefore come free, instead of Ernest Kingsbury, who has left the town.' Although the Attendance Officer appeared to inspect the register every week, there were a large number of absentees, mainly on account of the parents not being able to find the 2d per week, but also through children being kept away for employment on the land. Some of the children in out-of-the-way places do not seem to have been traced until it was nearly time for them to leave school. On 26 February 1889, the entry reads: 'Two children from the Fen admitted this morning. One is 10 years old and the other 9. They have not been to school before and do not know their letters.' There is an entry on 29th October, 1886, reading: 'Mary Gresswell has only been present 51 times out of a possible 154.'

This referred to my sister, and I once asked mother what was the cause of it. She explained that at this time the brother older than myself had just been born and, as mother was out at work, my sister had to stay at home to look after him and take him to her to be breast-fed twice a day.

I do not remember much about my early school years. I know that there were masters who came and went. One in particular was sufficiently eccentric for me to remember. At playtime in the morning he always went to the Red Lion for a drink, and it was well known that he spent his lunch time there. Very often in the afternoons he was 'indisposed', during which time we were entirely undisciplined and, so far as I remember, invariably went home. By this time there was an additional room built on to the school to accommodate the baby class. This was looked after by a young schoolmistress, but the big school was still very much overcrowded, and it was very difficult to divide the children into classes. I remember trying to learn only two poems. One was 'The Spanish Armada' the other 'Lucy Gray'. The whole school used to repeat a line after the teacher. This achieved very little result as far as memorising was concerned.

After the departure of the man who spent his time at the village pub there was a complete change, and there is no doubt that all pupils in the school at that time owe a very deep debt of gratitude to a conscientious and cultured man, a born schoolmaster, who took over at this juncture and stayed at the school long enough for many of us to secure a real and lasting benefit.

When Frederick Clow arrived, the school was in a deplorable condition from every aspect. The school managers had no funds and the education authorities had given notice that, unless there was a big improvement, the small grant would be withdrawn in three months. The children, myself included, knew practically nothing and were entirely without discipline. Mr Clow's previous salary had been £54 a year and a sum of £10 for the teaching of needlework out of which he had to provide an instructress. His duties included training the church choir and playing the harmonium twice at church on Sundays. His salary was the same at Digby, and he was to have the benefit of part of the grant from the Education authorities. Mrs Clow, both in the previous school and at Digby, taught the needlework, etc.

His first school day in Digby was a nightmare. The children came rushing into the place, jumped over desks, pushing and fighting like hooligans. It was impossible, even with shouting, to get any order, so that he decided to spend all the morning of the next day in marching them in and out of school until they could move in an orderly fashion. The only writing materials were slates and slate pencils, and the books necessary for teaching were practically non-existent. The first thing the schoolmaster did was to buy some exercise books, pens and ink and get rid of the slates. The educational standards were so low that the top standard could barely read and could not do the simplest arithmetic. I remember that at that time the schoolmaster's small child was brought out in front of us to give us demonstrations of how to do sums, etc.

At the end of the three months, after a visit by HM Inspectors, the school was given a reprieve and after six months the position was so improved that the grant was duly restored on a more permanent basis. During the day the schoolmaster was responsible for ninety children, including myself. He had one woman assistant and earned a salary of about £50 a year, together with a special State grant of £40 because it was a church school. He was the highest-paid man in the village. Next came the station-master, who earned about 30s a week, with house and uniform. His chief clerk received 21s. Platelayers working on the railway lines were much envied by other labourers since they got 16s a week and a half-holiday on Saturday.

There were sixty to seventy children in the one room, and it was only due to the hard work and ingenuity of the schoolmaster that they could be taught anything. The difficulty was that if he was taking one class, the other end of the school had to be kept quiet. One of his methods was to hang blackboards on the walls, on which he wrote lists of spellings. While one part of the school was otherwise occupied, the rest had to commit these words to memory.

He was not an orthodox teacher and was continually finding new ways to interest children. For instance, all the children had a passion for fox-hunting. In fact the only time I am mentioned in the log book is in an entry reading: 'Fred Gresswell went fox-hunting on Thursday.' It was quite customary for most of the children to stay away when the hounds met in the village. With the idea of inducing us to stay at school on this great morning, Mr Clow taught us hunting songs, which we were very willing to learn, and on the great day we all went to the Cross and sang lustily. After that we were given the rest of the day off.

This schoolmaster took an individual interest in every child, and if he or she had a bent it was encouraged and developed.

The author aged nine *(above)* and aged ninety *(right)*

The author's birthplace in Digby

Digby cross

I had not sufficient time to feel the full influence of this, but he worked hard on my two young brothers who were able to win scholarships, taking one to the Lincoln High School and the other to Sleaford Grammar School, a very big feat in those days in the village. He encouraged certain boys with few prospects here to emigrate to other countries, and one boy in particular, extremely difficult at school but with more than usual ability, later went to Australia and there became a member of Parliament.

He also started a night-school class in winter to teach the farm labourers to read and write. The fee was a penny a lesson, although the schoolmaster was no better off as the money was absorbed in lighting and heating the school. My father attended these classes. It caused quite a stir in the village to see middle-aged men wending their way to school with pencils and exercise books.

Mr Clow gave many of the children music lessons. In those days the great thing for the leisure evenings was either to sing or to play, and mother decided that I was to receive the benefit of this musical education, which was offered at 15s quarterly with lessons once a week. One day a harmonium arrived at the house. I am not certain whether it cost £3 or £5, but I was to be honoured by being the family musician.

It was one of the worst periods of my school life. I just could not learn to play; I hated the hours which I was supposed to spend practising and the lessons were a nightmare. My teacher almost tried to drive it into me with a poker, but nothing would go. The only result was that when, after two years, one Sunday morning the organist did not turn up, I was asked to officiate. I said I only knew two tunes, one Long Metre, the other Common Metre. That impressed them, but they wanted to know what hymns either of these would go with, and the one I chose was 'Praise Ye the Lord. 'Tis good to raise your hearts and voices in His praise.' I can remember starting the verse all right, but I invariably left the Sunday-school class to finish it. I was not asked again and that ended my career as a musician.

As a matter of interest, my younger brother, a born musician, only required two quarters' lessons for the schoolmaster to tell him that he was quite able to do all the rest himself. He later played the organ in one of the London churches.

One of the most pleasant and lasting of Mr Clow's efforts was the inauguration of the school concerts. This was an innovation. Nothing like it had been heard before. We had our sedate lantern lectures and sacred concerts at chapel and the same at the church, but Mr Clow introduced something with almost a music-hall flavour. He was taking a great risk, but it succeeded and provided a great deal of pleasure for the children and the parents. It certainly set to naught the primitive attempts by the older men at the Pig Club suppers.

We very quickly learned the songs and our respective parts in small plays. After the first concert it was only a question of how far the schoolmaster dare go. In my last year at school he decided to take a scene from Shakespeare. It was the trial scene from *The Merchant of Venice*. I was Shylock. (The schoolmaster may have been a good judge of character!) The one outstanding person was his own daughter, who played Portia. I had a sentimental regard for her, and I was more interested in her success than my own. I knew there were grave doubts about introducing Shakespeare in the village; ninety-nine out of a hundred people had never heard the name. Anyhow, it came off and was perhaps the greatest success of any of the concerts.

The subsequent history of Mr Clow was rather sad. He left Digby to take the headship of an industrial school in Lincoln. There he tried to apply the methods that had been successful with us, but his idea of winning the boys over did not succeed. They were too hard-bitten and eventually turned round and beat him up. This affected his health so much that he had to retire on the princely sum of £40 a year, which was the most he ever received up to the day of his death at eighty-five. His wife survived him for some years. Their only son was killed in the First World War.

He could discipline our village delinquents successfully enough. I recall him bringing a boy out to the front of the class and saying: 'You seem to know a lot about cycles. How much blood is there in a bicycle wheel?' He had heard the lad use the forbidden word in the playground in referring to that part of his machine.

It is a queer thought that Mr Clow's improvement of the standard of local education was not wholly approved by the ultra-conservatives. In fact, one of the big farmers, himself a school manager, complained to the schoolmaster that he was over-educating the children. They were getting above themselves and were inclined to laugh at some of the illiterate local preachers. This local bigwig failed to realise that by offering seasonal employment in the fields to schoolchildren, he was completely upsetting the educational programme he had been elected to support.

4
GETTING ON

If you have built castles in the air, your work need not be lost; that is where they should be. Now put the foundations under them.

THOREAU

Every Saturday I did the shopping for Miss Biddy Brown. It sometimes took two hours, and she paid me a halfpenny for doing it. This was her standard rate of payment. I remember on one occasion she employed two boys to fetch a dolly tub and a peggy from a quarter of a mile down the street. (A dolly tub was a wash-tub for clothes and a peggy was a wooden contraption used for dunking and swirling the clothes in the tub.) After struggling with these unwieldy objects the boys expected at least a halfpenny each, but she escaped by taking them both to the shop and buying just a halfpenny-worth of sweets to be shared between the two of them.

Miss Brown's order was not a big one, but it could take as much as an hour to make up. I knew the list by heart. The follow-items were always included: ¼lb Mazawatte tea, 2lb soft sugar, ½lb large tea biscuits, 1oz thick twist for George, 1oz shag for Charlie, 3 boxes of matches (1d), ½gall of paraffin. On some occasions she also included 1 bar of white soap, 1 penny tin of blacking, 1 packet of wax candles and 1 packet of Van Houten's cocoa, as well as Miss Biddy's one extravagance – a penny bar of plain chocolate, and perhaps other small items.

The reason it took so long was that all the grown-ups were attended to in-between. It could cause even more delay if I had to go to the drapery counter for a penny packet of pins or a reel of cotton. There would be sure to be a customer in front of me who would be buying, say, 3yd of union shirting or flannelette.

Miss Brown lived in Digby until the age of ninety-four. Not long before her death the cottage she had occupied all her life fell into a bad state of decay and was scheduled for demolition. Miss Brown said she would sooner go with the house than move. In a sense she did, for, though finally prevailed on to move to a nearby cottage, she died a few weeks later.

Another of my freelance jobs at that time was to wheel out an invalid paying guest who lived at the village store. For this I was paid 2d an hour. She was quite 15 stone, and while it was not very hilly country, I remember that pushing her chair was hard work when the roads were muddy, for there were no tar roads in those days. She caused me considerable embarrassment once when a man came by leading a large shire stallion, decorated with gaily coloured ribbons. She asked me what these horses were used for; they never seemed to do any work. I remember the difficulty I had in evading the question.

More profitable than these jobs, indeed my most profitable job, was 'flagging', at the rate of 3d for short journeys and 6d for long ones (ie over two miles) for my uncle. He had a set of threshing tackle which had to be moved every day or two, and the regulation at that time was that a steam-engine was allowed on the road only on condition that someone went in front with a flag to lead oncoming horses past the engine. If the flagger was too small, as I was, the man on the machine had to get out and do it.

From the time I was eight years old I had to get up at six o'clock every morning in summer to take the cows two miles to the Ashby field. This and the home paddock, a total of 4 acres, was our grazing land for seven cows. The 6-acre field was the meadow land. Apart from the distance away the worst feature of the Ashby field was that we had to go another mile to draw water from a well to water the cows.

When I got back from this early morning job, I had my breakfast and then took milk round the village before going to school at nine o'clock. At lunch time there was always plenty to do, chopping mangolds, fetching water for the cows, and so on. After school, I went to fetch the cows back. Later we worked in the garden or on the allotments rented by small-holders from the Council to provide root crops for the cows, corn for pig-meal, and potatoes for themselves. The big day for work was Saturday, when some extra jobs were waiting to be done, such as setting and picking potatoes, singling mangolds, and, in the summer, hay-making and harvesting.

If we were short of grass, Saturdays in summer could be very pleasant. I had all the morning to take the cows to the field, so that they would graze by the wayside and fill their bellies on other people's frontages. Part of the etiquette of driving cows was to keep them on the move and not 'tent' them (allow them to graze on the verges). If we had no grass in our fields I was allowed to let the two-mile journey take all morning, but had strict instructions to take them straight back on the principle that it is wrong to tent cows when their bellies are full. During this ambling with the cows I used to build my castles in the air. It must have been during one of these daydreams that I thought out my scheme to make a million pounds by the time I was twenty-one. This project had a sequence which I shall mention later.

One of my jobs on a Saturday morning in the summer time was spudding thistles in the field where I took the cows. A spud is a long-handled spade with which you dig thistles out of the ground. In those days it was customary for the farmer walking round his fields to use a spud as a walking stick and, occasionally for exercise, dig one up.

I found it a tedious and lonely job, and on one occasion I thought if I could get another boy to help me I could probably clear the small field and have time to spare for playing about. I possessed a halfpenny which I was prepared to invest in labour for this purpose. There was a boy about my own age who was very poor, but not a particularly reliable character. When I mentioned the project to him the great point with him was: when would he touch the money?

I made the first mistake by suggesting that I would buy sweets and he could have them while he was working. Unfortunately, on the two-mile journey with the cows he had already finished the sweets by half way and was turning for home. I had to think quickly, and on the spur of the moment I offered an inducement which in my own mind I thought was a million to one chance against. It was that if we killed a rabbit he could have it. He accepted this offer and, strange to say, such a thing had never happened before, but we had not been working five minutes before he put his spud straight through the neck of a rabbit sitting amongst a clump of grass and thistles. Of course he was delighted with this and at once made off home with the spoils.

I had to toil all day and return home at night to find that the news had already preceded me to my mother. Although she claimed that I had no authority to make the bargain she would not trust to rumours, and it was only when I had to confess that it was true that she set out to demand the rabbit from the boy's mother. But she, sensing what would happen, and knowing my mother, said it was too late as the rabbit was already in the pot! The only part she managed to salvage was the skin.

During one Christmas holiday I worked for a week scaring crows for 8d a day on a farm where my father was employed. The field, known as 'the 40 acre', was at the back of beyond, about a mile from the road. To scare the crows I had wooden clappers that made a considerable noise. Unfortunately, the crows soon got used to them and took no notice, so then I had to chase them up and down the field with a stick. The only means I had of knowing the time to go home was to watch for the departure of the shepherd penning sheep two fields away.

One night I missed him during my running about, and it got gradually darker and darker. I was some two miles from home and feeling very lonely when, to my intense relief, I saw my father coming to look for me.

What I liked best about the shepherd was his hut. I was always warm inside there, and he could actually fry bacon and potatoes on an oil-stove. I have never tasted anything more appetising than this dish after a long day in the fields.

Other days are well remembered. In the shooting season we used to go beating for 1s a day, with sandwiches and beer provided for lunch. On my first day I was unfortunate in having a hare shot in front of me. It was nearly as big as myself, and I had to carry it for more than an hour over ploughed fields until we came to the game cart.

The most pleasant day was when the Blankney Hunt met in the village and the schoolmaster got us to sing 'A-Hunting We Will Go' at the village cross before the hounds moved off. It went like this:

> Farmer Hodge to his dame said 'I am 60 and lame,
> Times are hard yet my rent I must pay,
> But I don't care a jot if I raise it or not
> For I must go a-hunting today.
> All Nature looks smiling and gay,
> So let's join the glad throng that goes laughing along
> And we'll all go a-hunting today.'

As the hunt moved off we were allowed to follow the hounds. For the first time in my life I knew what easy money was. For opening a gate for one of the 'redcoats' who had a groom in attendance I was given a shilling. Later in the day I shared another gate-opening with a boy, thus making 1s 6d for the day. It was the quickest and easiest money I had ever received.

Before I reached the phase of making 'easy money' by casual jobs I experienced the main difficulty confronting the ambitious beginner. It was necessary to find the sum of 3d to start myself in a one-man business. It was produced in this way.

Our main connection with the outside world, at least from the literary point of view, was through a weekly newspaper called the *Lincolnshire Chronicle,* still flourishing and influential. The only other paper was the *Christian Herald,* and I was always fascinated by the advertisements that appeared in this latter journal, particularly those addressed to people eager to start in business for themselves.

One advertisement that particularly tempted me was connected with the jewellery business. The advertiser offered to send jewellery which could be either sold or returned. For some reason three penny stamps were needed and, as I knew it would be useless to ask my parents for 3d, I started roaming the fields to collect bones for the rag-and-bone merchant in the village. I could not get enough this way, but with the help of a rabbit skin which I came across, I managed to raise the necessary capital and in due course received cards of rolled gold cuff-links, brooches, and so on. I can particularly remember the brooches, as they were the only two things I sold, at 1s 6d each, and the sale was made to a relative who had recently come into money. The commission was about 6d.

I then wrote to Cochrane's Fent Warehouse in Manchester, and they sent me a catalogue. (Fents are remnants of cloth.) On the frontispiece was a striking slogan: 'There was once a man who for fifteen years was confined to a dark and loathsome dungeon. One day a happy thought struck him. He opened the window and got out.'

I was ten when I read this, and thought to myself that I still had five years left.

It was necessary first to send the money for these parcels of fents, which were made up in 10s lots. According to the catalogue they were priced at half the normal retail rates. I took this catalogue round the village and collected the money in advance. When the parcel arrived, all my customers unfortunately wanted the same lots, which were obviously offered in the advertisement to attract custom. Nobody wanting the residue, there was no profit.

I tried one short cut to wealth in my early struggles which caused me some embarrassment. A firm advertised in a weekly paper, offering a prize of £70 for solving a puzzle which included a saying: 'All is not gold that glitters.' In this case it was a very appropriate quotation, as I found out later.

There was no entrance fee, and I sent my solution and in due course received an intimation that I was a winner. I took this to mean *the* winner, and unfortunately told some boys on my way to school. Very quickly it was all round the village, and I was congratulated by the schoolmaster. It was later, when we studied the conditions for receiving the prize, that there came a doubt that all might not be well. I was required to send 3s 6d for some sort of book and the prize would be forwarded. My parents noted that I was only a winner, and they couldn't see any reason why the

3s 6d could not be deducted from the £70. Much to my disappointment they refused to allow me to send the money. Later we heard that someone else in the district had also been a winner and had sent 3s 6d. This entrant got a worthless book and a ½d postage stamp as his share of the winnings!

We were innocent people in Lincolnshire in those days.

One memorable day soon after this an advertisement appeared in the *Christian Herald,* reading: 'Bright boys wanted, no capital. Apply Colporteur Department, 24 Tudor Street, London.' Here was something in which I thought I could claim to have both qualifications. I immediately replied to the advertisement, and by return received twelve copies (free) of the current issue of the *Sunday Companion.* I was asked to sell them at 1d each and return the proceeds. The commission on this would be 4d. What surprises me, even to this day, is why the *Christian Herald* published such an advertisement from a rival concern, because the obvious thing for me was to sell my first copy of the *Companion* to my parents, who immediately cancelled the *Herald.*

I read the *Sunday Companion* through and started a door-to-door canvass of the village. Fortunately, that issue contained the first instalment of a new serial by the very popular novelist, Silas K. Hocking, and I emphasised this in my patter. I also gave the names of all the other special writers and described the subjects of their articles. It was not until late at night, after I had covered three villages, that I eventually arrived home, every copy sold. I brought with me 1s – and made the mistake of sending this sum back in full to pay for the next week's issue.

In due course I received eighteen copies, and this rather knocked the breath out of me. However I was able to retain most of my first week's customers, and I borrowed from them copies of the previous issue, containing the first instalment of the serial, to use as an inducement to new customers. By canvassing two more villages I managed to sell all eighteen. For the next week's supply I sent only 1s to the publishers and emphasised the point that eighteen was the maximum I could hope to sell. In their reply they suggested that I might be able to sell other periodicals which they owned, and they sent me some sample copies of 1d novelettes published weekly. These were *Golden Stories, Sunday Stories, Penny Stories* and *Pocket Library*. As I did not want to overload my *Sunday Companion* circulation I decided to try the mansions in the district. I read the sample copies through, and left copies with the maids at these big houses on the understanding that I would get them back if I received no order.

I was agreeably surprised to find how well they were received. Moreover, I was able to sell them in some ordinary houses along with the *Sunday Companion*. They became a drug with one young woman, who used to spend up to 2s weekly of the 15s that her husband earned. I got my total sales very quickly up to six dozen a week. This realised 2s in commission, as much as a man's wage for a day's work. By this time I had graduated to the bright boots class, and was given certain privileges which made life more pleasant. During the last winter at home I occupied the best bedroom, and was allowed the hitherto unheard of luxury of having a coal fire in the bedroom once a week in the winter. This was on a Wednesday night when my stock of periodicals arrived. These I read right through before delivering them on the Saturday.

The sales manager of the *Lincoln Leader*, hearing of my success, approached me to see if I could sell their paper on my round. It was a Liberal newspaper and our constituency was a stronghold of Conservatism. In fact our Member was the local squire the Hon H. H. Chaplin, and a cabinet minister at that. This newspaper was looked upon with general suspicion. The total circulation in my particular district was six a week. I accepted the agency, however, and, as with the books, read each issue right through.

The paper sent an official canvasser to go round with me. Before the first morning was out I had learnt his patter. We went from door to door and said: 'I represent the *Lincoln Leader*, the paper with the latest and most up-to-date news. Special correspondents have been appointed in the district to report on all local sporting and social events. The paper contains many interesting features, including a gossip column entitled "Around the Village Pump", and also a new series on "Health and Home", by Dr Gordon Stables. We have doubled our circulation in the last three months, and now we are increasing on the increase.'

I did not know what the last sentence meant, but it seemed to round off the appeal nicely.

I increased the circulation of the *Lincoln Leader* in my district to a very shaky sixty. That is to say, Mr Chaplin or one of his supporters had only to make a disparaging reference to the paper and the circulation might drop to twenty. Also, the village news was really not covered as well as it was in the *Lincolnshire Chronicle*. I therefore proposed that I should do the reporting for my area.

This suggestion was accepted, and at a ½d a line I was prepared to swamp them with news. Whether this rocked their boat financially, or the stuff was not suitable for publication, only a small amount was inserted. Nevertheless, my revenue from the *Lincoln Leader* sales and reporting fees, together with my commission from the *Sunday Companion,* brought me in a total income of 5s a week. Once the initial canvassing was over, my paper round by bicycle occupied about four hours altogether each Saturday.

It has always been rather on my conscience that I may have been sowing the seeds of Squire Chaplin's eventual defeat at the polls. Some years later, to everybody's surprise, he was beaten by a Liberal candidate. I remember the gloom that descended on the village. It was as though the world was coming to an end, and, as a matter of fact, perhaps it was the beginning of the end of that particular world.

At the time I said to my mother, 'What difference will it make to us?' and she replied: 'I don't see how it will make any difference. It has always been bed and work for the likes of us, and will always be bed and work.' As Parnell said to the cheering roadman: 'Ireland shall have her freedom but you will still break stones.'

5
COUNTRY CHILDHOOD

Oh, is the water sweet and cool,
Gentle and brown, above the pool?
And laughs the immortal river still
Under the mill, under the mill?
Say, is there beauty yet to find?
And Certainty? and Quiet kind?
Deep meadows, yet, for to forget
The lies, the truths, and pain? . . . Oh! yet
Stands the Church clock at ten to three?
And is there honey still for tea?

RUPERT BROOKE

The date of the village school holidays was governed by the harvest. The idea was that all the children would then go to work in the fields, so that it was an exciting day when someone broke the news that Bell was opening out at the far meadows. Had we heard that any of the other farmers had started we should have known that it was only a rumour; Bell was always the first to start. There was an extra note of excitement when we rose to begin morning school by singing:

Fair waved the golden corn
In Canaan's pleasant land,
When full of joy some shining morn
Went forth the reaper's band.

From the school window we could see in the distance the man with the scythe opening out the field ready for the reaper, and we knew that the holidays would be starting within a day or two.

In my early days there was a certain amount of work for children in the harvest fields where they had reapers only. The parents would gather and stook the corn at so much the acre; the children's job was to make the bands with which their parents bound the sheaves. After the corn had been led most of the women and children came to glean from the stubble. In the normal way they would get sufficient to feed the family pig during the winter. Quite early in my life the reaper gave place to the binder, and the stubble was picked too clean to make it worth while to do very much in the way of gleaning.

Nevertheless, this established custom continued for many years, even though there was little in the way of pickings. As a child I was fascinated by the occupation for two reasons. One was that the only romance which interested me in the Bible was that of Ruth, and even today I look at the harvest field and think of the 'sad heart of Ruth when sick for home she stood in tears amid the alien corn'. The other was that it was the only occasion I knew on which you could take other people's property with impunity.

It was recognised that you could trespass on the farmer's property and gather everything that was left on the ground. It was, of course, understood that, if you were connected with anyone who had any land of their own, you were not morally entitled to glean, and young as I was, I realised that I was committing a breach of social etiquette. Even so, I persuaded my mother to provide me with a pillow case and a bag-apron and tried to lose myself in the small crowd of women and children who wended their way to the fields every morning. Unfortunately they had perambulators and various other conveyances to bring back the spoils at night time, whilst I had to struggle with them on my head or as best I could. I don't think that anything I was able to gather provided one pig with food for a week.

The other free concession also supplied exciting entertainment. Everybody had the right to kill rabbits in the harvest field. The great thing was to finish the last part of a field in one day because as the binder went round, the rabbits gathered in the centre until finally you could walk down the side of the corn and see them lying there, very easy to knock over.

The gamekeeper was always at hand to see that no game was killed, but occasionally you would see men as they were walking down the side hit at something which they did not stoop to pick up, and you would know that it was a rabbit with feathers on it. They would wait for the binder to come to gather up the sheaf, and afterwards, when the gamekeeper had gone home, they would go back and collect the choice pheasant.

Everybody gathered round for the last load coming into the farm, and then there would be a harvest supper. This consisted mainly of rabbit pies and plenty of beer with singing.

In our house money was scarcer than food. I well remember that my father never carried any money about with him for fear he should lose it, though mother was always insisting that he should take something. In the end he said he would carry a shilling, and she said: 'That's just as silly as having nothing. What can you do with more than 3d?' Money was not carried in purses, but in linen bags bigger than tobacco pouches. The bag was folded up and rolled to put into the pocket. One shilling in such a bag would have been like a needle in a haystack.

My parents were sensible in allowing us to keep anything we earned though we had to buy necessities with our own money. When I started a book-round, for example, I had to buy my own clothes, and, as it was essential to my job, my first bicycle. It was a solid-tyred bone-shaker and I paid 10s for it.

The first person I saw riding on wheels was my brother, who had bought a penny-farthing bicycle. It had a large front wheel with a seat on top, and a tiny wheel at the back. He came home from Ancaster, ten miles away, and gave me a short ride. I was only three or four, and perched precariously on the seat, felt myself at a great height above the ground. It needed a strong man to exceed walking pace on this contraption.

After this came the bone-shaker. In shape it was very much like the modern type, but the tyres were solid. Three-wheelers also began to appear. These were slow-moving, but people had got the idea that a bad ride was better than a good walk, and I heard a man boast that he had ridden one of them from Ashby to Digby in a bare three-quarters of an hour. This was a distance of two miles that one would normally walk in half an hour.

About that time my father bought his first new, cushion-tyred, safety bicycle for 25s 9d. The negotiations started at about five in the evening, when the price was 26s 6d. While this was going on, I had to go on an errand. I returned an hour later, and I was still hanging around at about nine o'clock when the final price was agreed. My interest had a practical side, because I received 3d 'lucky money' – the final amount to be knocked off the price.

The great ambition of all village people, when they emerged from the labouring classes, was to have a pony and trap. It was thus a memorable occasion in my boyhood when, completely out of the blue, my father appeared one day with a small pony and trap, the total cost of which must have been £7 or £8.

I have never known whether this was to establish our prestige on having reached the small-holding stage, or whether my parents had in mind that they could make the pony earn its keep by hiring it out. I must have been about eight at this time and, as it was winter and I had no cows to fetch, I was immediately given the job of driving the pony to bring father from work.

He was still working as a labourer at Ashby-de-la-Launde. It was entered from plain open country, through an avenue of trees, the gateway to which was an arch known as 'The Lordship'. The inhabitants were mostly retainers attached to the Hall. There were houses for the gamekeepers, woodmen, coachmen and gardeners, and a very dignified detached house for the butler.

On Sunday mornings I sometimes accompanied father on the long walk to Ashby Church, where he was one of the bell-ringers. Before going into church I used to wait for the procession from the Hall as this was very impressive. The Hall was about a quarter of a mile from the church and between the two points there was a well-kept walk, banked with thick hedges which joined overhead. Halfway between the Hall and the church this path was crossed by the road. The squire of Ashby was a bachelor, Captain N. H. Reeve King. He started off from the Hall in front of a procession in which the housekeeper and butler went first, followed by the servants in their proper order. (At that time he had about six maids.) At the junction with the road they were joined for the rest of the way by the outdoor servants. On the occasions when I had to go, I always joined the procession there.

Mr and Mrs Clow: schoolmaster and schoolmistress

The author, aged twenty-two, during World War I

The author's future wife, May, at the age of eighteen

I actually spoke to the Captain only once, and that was when I attended the village feast.

This was a very tiny affair compared with ours, but on this particular day, as a gesture, a cheap-jack was allowed to bring his barrow outside the Hall grounds and erect a stall with the usual children's games and presents. I remember feeling rather an outsider among a small group of about twelve children who were standing around with nothing to do. Apparently, however, they were waiting for the Captain and he came along with his gold-headed cane and bought most of the toys. These he distributed one by one to the children. I was feeling rather embarrassed, when, to my surprise, he recognised me and included me among his beneficiaries.

Mention of the cheap-jack reminds me that watches were most important things in the villagers' life. It was every boy's ambition to own one and, later on, one's watch became the symbol of one's wealth and respectability. You knew a man by the sort of watch he wore, and of course the chain always corresponded. The boastful man would wear a big watch and chain to match. The thriftless man, if he had one, usually had a cheap one that was very uncertain in its timekeeping, if it went at all. These were usually bought from cheap-jacks at 3s 9d to 5s each. As the status of a man, and indeed a woman, improved, so did the quality of his or her watch. Many a poor family could boast of heirlooms which indicated that at one time they, or their families, had been better off. By our standards the great thing was to own a silver watch.

Only the gentry sported gold watches, although a great-aunt of ours was the proud possessor of perhaps the only one in the village. This watch caused a bitter feud which split our family for a lifetime; even today the descendants regard each other with uneasy suspicion.

It started with the great-aunt's daughter marrying against her mother's wishes. She, by way of revenge, gave the much-coveted watch to my mother, who was a favourite niece. Mother was naturally pleased at the time, but later it turned out to be a very troublesome and expensive gift, and only served to prove her contention that something for nothing is never worth while.

Everybody in the village knew that mother had been given the watch, and the consensus of opinion was that, whether the daughter should have it or not, mother was not entitled to it.

This happened before I was born, but the vibrations from the controversy still echoed in the village, and although I knew little about the facts I did know that there was a barrier between the families. The daughter had a large family contemporary with ours. We all went to school and Sunday-school together, and although they were quite friendly children, we did not mix outside school hours.

One day, like a bolt from the blue, hostilities flared up with a vengeance. Mother got a solicitor's letter demanding the return of the watch; the other daughter had been found to be legally entitled to it. It appeared that the great-aunt had died some time before, and later her husband died leaving everything to his daughter. As the Married Women's Property Act stood at that time, the watch became the property of her husband. Mother refused to give it up on the grounds that Aunt had always owned the watch, and she had evidence to prove it had been given to her.

The case eventually went to Court and was the *cause célèbre* of my generation, the battle being fought to a finish. The result was that mother lost, the plaintiff establishing her claim. Mother also had to pay £5 court fees. It was the only time in which I ever knew mother proved to be in the wrong, and even in this case she could claim a moral right.

To continue, Captain Reeve King was an aristocrat of the old school. He wore an eye-glass and was chief magistrate for the district. He attended the market town of Sleaford, seven miles away, once or twice a week and drove in his carriage-and-pair with coachman and footman, to Digby Station where he was met again in the afternoon.

As they returned home the carriage-and-pair often passed me in the pony and trap on the Ashby road. This was a matter of anxiety for the coachman, as I did not have very much control over the pony. He never knew which side the animal would decide to take, and the road was lined with ditches. If it was anywhere I could stop I did so, but it very often happened that the footman had to get down and lead my pony to the side himself.

On two occasions the pony was nearly the death of me. Quite apart from the trouble with the squire's carriage-and-pair, this journey held another hidden menace.

Two miles beyond Ashby on the heath, up by the London ramper (the old Roman road to London), there was a farm known as Temple Bruer. It was on the site of an old monastery. The isolated compound of this estate always had a sinister effect on my mind because, although I could see it from the road across the field, I never came into friendly touch with any of the inhabitants.

So wild and lonely was this part of the world that there was a remarkable land lighthouse there called Dunston Pillar, which in the old days was used to guide travellers on the heath.

Several times a week the Temple Bruer team had to come to Digby Station with corn. This they brought down in two or three wagon-loads at a time, each drawn by four powerful shire horses with a man riding one of the near-side horses of the last pair.

They sounded like phantoms rattling their chains. They went straight to the station, delivered their goods, turned round and started for home at a gallop, and the thundering hooves of the great shire horses vibrated through the village. I was always instructed to get the pony very quickly out of the way if they were in the vicinity. One day, however, with only about 1,000yd downhill to go to the place where father was working, I heard the roar of hooves behind me in the distance and thinking I could make it, I whipped the pony on; but on the way down the pony, whether from fright or not I do not know, stumbled and fell to its knees.

By this time the horses and wagons were nearly on top of us, and I could almost feel the breath of the horses on my neck. Although the pony had fallen before, it had never previously been able to get up until the shafts had been removed. If the same thing had happened on this occasion we should both have been killed. By a miracle, however, the pony, with a tremendous effort, got to its feet in time to go ahead of the wagons. This experience taught me never to try racing Temple Bruer horses.

I could drive this particular pony, but he would not let me

ride him on long journeys; he insisted on lying down as soon as I got on his back. On one occasion, when he had lain down three times soon after I had mounted, I rode him to the village pond for a drink. To my consternation he walked into the pond and stood there. There was a big well in the middle and we were only a foot or two away from it. None of the villagers dared to come in, in case they frightened the pony into the well, so we all just had to wait until, eventually, the pony solved the problem himself by lying down in the water. Several villagers rushed in and brought me out.

When I fetched my father from work with the pony and trap, we always had a passenger going home. He was a man called Bugg, who worked on the same farm as my father. He was a pensioned soldier, straight as a ramrod, and a bachelor. When he first came to Digby he was considered very eligible, for he was reputed to be worth £200 and a wagon-load of furniture. His pension of about 5s a week enhanced his prestige. But he had the reputation of being rather mean, and though we gave him a lift night and morning, the only time he gave me anything was at Christmas when I received 1s. This seemed a lot of money all at once, but there was a long time to wait in between.

At the same time he was very careful not to give the impression of begging for a lift. Every time we had to get into the trap he always started walking down the road in front of us, and when we caught him up, my father would say: 'Now mate you might as well ride.' To this he would reply: 'Well if it's the same to you.' The situation was a little awkward about harvest-time, because we usually got a lot of rabbits, and loading up a couple of dozen rabbits in a small trap besides three people was no easy matter.

There was one occasion when Bugg might have regretted his free ride. After the episode with the Temple Bruer's wagon, the pony was definitely nervous whenever these teams came within earshot. In fact, when I was alone I would get down and hold him until the wagons had passed. One night on our way home we heard the rumble of their approach. The pony pricked his ears and started moving faster for home. My father did not take much notice at first, but the pony really began to gallop, kicking the dashboard with his heels. And then an unfortunate thing happened – one rein broke. Bugg, who usually sat stiffly upright, leaned over and grabbed the lamp-bracket, but it came away in his hands. The pony stumbled and fell; we were thrown out on the side of the road, suffering some bruises but nothing more, and it was the pony that got the worst of it.

I seem to have been born to have trouble with ponies, as a later chapter will confirm. Another of my boyish adventures is still a nightmare.

I had heard some discussion between my parents and the shepherd where father worked. Apparently the shepherd wanted to borrow our pony and trap to take his wife and family for a few days' holiday to Navenby. This village was about eight miles from Ashby by road, and to go by rail necessitated their coming to Digby Station and making a detour of some twenty miles. I was the only person available to go with them to bring the pony, Tommy, and trap back. It was thought that the journey both ways would take about four to five hours, and I duly set off one morning to Ashby to pick them up.

In the normal way the two miles journey to Ashby was the extent of the pony's travels, except on the odd occasions he had been to Sleaford, and when he reached the shepherd's home he naturally thought he was at the end of his journey. As the trap was loaded up he started to look more and more dejected, and when he set out on a new road he was obviously bewildered and depressed. Fortunately Shep, as we called him, had been given instructions to drive the pony on the outward journey, as it was not expected that he would cause any trouble once he had turned his head towards home. It was quite a big weight on Tommy's back and no doubt more on his mind when we set off with the man and his wife, three children, myself and the luggage.

This was new country to me. After going about a mile we turned on to the old ramper road from Lincoln to Sleaford. We followed this for half a mile to Brauncewell Church and then turned right over the heath by a long, straight road of about four miles. At this stage I also became depressed. I had been accustomed in driving round our immediate vicinity, to be surrounded by friendly hedges and a village every mile or so with plenty of homes in between, but here was desolate country. Hedges had been replaced by walls, and one could look for miles without seeing a house. What was worse still, there were hills to be negotiated. In the past, we had usually got out and walked at anything in the way of a rise in the ground, and the same downhill, but Shep did not know this, and I did not like to say anything. It was only by the use of the whip that we got up the hills, and I could see it was taking the pony all its time to keep on its feet going down.

I was beginning to feel sorry that I had started this journey, but I had not taken into account the pony, who had apparently been making up his mind on some drastic action. Down a very steep hill, near the bottom, with the idea of giving some impetus for going up the next one, Shep brought his whip out, and to my surprise the pony started to gallop. This went on for about 100yd when he suddenly fell down and shot the whole lot of us out on the road. Fortunately, I fell on the grass verge, and so did the driver, but from the screaming of both his wife and children it was obvious that somebody was severely hurt. With the children it was mainly shock, but Shep's wife was very much cut and bruised and had broken her wrist. I ran back to a farmhouse about a mile away and somebody came with a cart to take the family to the house. That was the end of the holiday so far as they were concerned.

I turned the pony homewards. The blood was oozing from his knees, and he was obviously in pain, but his step was lighter. Unfortunately, I had to pass my father on the way back. I was walking with the pony, and we were a long way off, when I saw him. As we got nearer he must have seen the broken knees of the pony. I shouted out: 'It wasn't me, I wasn't driving.'

What everybody had overlooked in making the arrangements was that Tommy had acquired the technique of falling down in any emergency. It is well known that ponies and horses, once they have broken their knees, lose confidence and are never the same afterwards. We parted company with Tommy soon after.

6
FIRST STEPS ALONE

O'erjoy'd was he to find
That though on pleasure she was bent,
She had a frugal mind.

COWPER

My previous reference to the importance of watches in a rural community irresistibly recalls my first encounter with our local 'Watch King' and, much more poignantly, the circumstances of an outing that made a deep impression on my mind.

I was eight or nine when I had my first day's holiday alone. Sleaford was our nearest market town, six and a half miles away from Digby. I had been several times to the market with my father when we had pigs for sale. We always reckoned that, by pony and trap, it took exactly an hour from leaving home to Sleaford Workhouse, which was on the outskirts.

On one occasion we set off to go to the market but never got there. On Sunday, the previous day, I had been very pleased to be told by my father that I would have to go with him to market the next day as we had a litter of eight pigs and the trap, being a small one, needed someone to help keep them in. Unfortunately for me, when he got to within two miles of Sleaford, on the Ruskington road, we were waylaid by two men who came out of the hedge bottom. They asked to have a look at the pigs, explaining they were going to the market to buy some, and suggesting it might be a saving to both if we could do a deal.

One of them asked father how much he was expecting to get and he replied: 'They were making 21s last week.' The men looked at each other and shook their heads. One said: 'Did you see the price at Lincoln last Friday? Suckling pigs were a poor market, lucky to get 19s.' After some discussion they said they would 'middle it' and give £1 a head. Father thought about it and then said: 'No we have come so far we may as well see what the auction is like.' I was feeling relieved as we started off, but we had only gone a few yards when one of the men shouted after us: 'Just a minute, I'll tell you what we'll do, we'll make it £1 and 6d a head. You'll save that and you'll save buying your dinner,' – he looked at me – 'and the boy's dinner, and you'll save putting up the pony and trap.' Up to this point, the argument did not seem to affect father, but the man continued: 'And what is more you will be able to go back to your work.' Father did not understand much about business, but he always thought it a waste of time to have to go to Sleaford, and the thought of going straight back to work clinched the deal. There was the usual argument about 'lucky money' – they wanted 2s 6d but eventually agreed on 1s. We handed over the pigs and turned round for home.

It was a sad journey back because I knew I should have to go to school in the afternoon, and father was worried as to what mother would say. When the story was told she said: 'Well, I shouldn't have done it, but we'll see what the paper says on Saturday.' Woe was it to father when the market price disclosed that the price had gone up to 22s a head. As mother said: 'There's an 8s dead loss whichever way you look at it, and you've never earned 8s in two days, much less in half a day.'

I had always wanted to go to Sleaford for the May Monday Fair – Plough Monday. This was the day when the yearly hirings took place for the farm-hands who lived in the farmhouse. There were 'boys', aged between twelve and sixteen, then 'seconds', aged between sixteen and twenty, and then wagoners, from twenty years upwards. They all had to be unmarried. Most of the young people went, whether they were seeking a job or staying on. My parents gave me permission to go on the understanding that I was to see what was happening without spending any money. I naturally looked forward to the day for several weeks before, and on the Sunday preceding, a wet and blustery day, I went down to the Village Cross to talk to the young people who would be going.

The better-class farms usually fixed up their hirelings before May Day. It was the roughest type of place and the poorest type of men that left making a bargain until the last minute. This was concluded by the simple process of the employer giving the servant 5s 'fasten penny', which constituted a legal contract. They carried 5s pieces about for this purpose.

At the Cross I asked one young man: 'Will you go if it rains?' He looked at me in disgust. 'I shall go if it rains muck-forks', he said. It was still raining the next morning when I set out. After much discussion it was decided that 9d would be a reasonable sum to spend, out of which I had to pay my railway fare, 4½d at half price. The village station was crowded and when the train came in it was packed. I managed to creep into a carriage that already had fifteen young men. All of them were smoking, and although it was only a short journey of less than seven miles, I was feeling sickly by the time I arrived.

My parents had suggested to me that if I went direct to the Black Bull, kept by my Aunt Emma and her husband Uncle George, I might be invited to dinner. If so, I could stay until a later train and spend the 4½d as I wished. This seemed to be the most important business, so I went straight to the Black Bull. They always provided an 'ordinary' on market days. For 9d one could have a plate of beef, mutton or pork, together with vegetables, and bread and cheese afterwards, although it was usual to order a pint of threepenny beer with it. Of course it was half-price for children, but this would have absorbed all my cash.

May Monday was the busiest day of the year for public-houses and I suppose I was not very welcome. However, my aunt invited me to the beer cellar where they could have a word with me as they were drawing beer. Unfortunately, the combined effect of the smoke in the train, together with the rank smell of beer, resulted in my being horribly sick. My aunt suggested I should get some fresh air, but she invited me to come back for dinner. Having been thus relieved in mind and body, I proceeded to see the sights. First, I went to the fun fair, although I was not tempted to spend any money as it would apparently have gone too quickly. But I was fortunate in being offered a free ride on the roundabouts by a girl from the village, who had been at school and was home after her first year in domestic service. The side-shows intrigued me, but I decided to look round before parting with any money.

I then went to the market place and thoroughly enjoyed listening to the patter of the cheap-jacks. I was fortunate that the most celebrated of them all was present that day. His name was Charlie Lidget, and he was known as the 'Watch King'. His name was a household word in our village. He was no ordinary cheap-jack; he owned a jeweller's shop in Lincoln and was known to give value for money. He came from agricultural stock and was quite at home among farm workers. Moreover, he was one of Lincolnshire's great comics, and he always had a crowd of people because of his entertainment value.

He had once been to the Red Lion Inn at Digby. I remember one of the things he was offering was a special line in braces. He said he wore them himself, and to test their strength he had stood with one foot on Lincoln Minster and the other on Boston Stump; he bent down and in doing so touched the moon with his backside, and drank out of the sea at Skegness – and the braces stood the strain!

He had just opened out when I arrived, and was in a serious mood befitting a special day when there was big money about. He explained that he had bought a big consignment of special watches of the highest quality; these he described in detail, laying special emphasis on the fact that they were jewelled in every movement. He said that the normal price of these watches was £5, but that was not his price. He was not going to charge £4, not even £3. Two pounds was his price. Then he said, 'But wait a minute, this is your lucky day. I have some special news for you which is confidential', and he told us that recently a cutlery manufacturer with whom he did business had got into low water financially. To tide him over, he had taken from him a large quantity of stock at give-away prices, and he proposed to pass on the benefits of this wonderful bargain to his customers.

To every buyer of a £2 watch he was going to make a present of a carving knife and fork. He then turned to his assistant and said: 'And what about throwing in something else?' His man replied by protesting it would be going too far, and I myself began to feel that he would be losing money. There was then an argument as to who was the man and who was the boss until, finally, Charlie said: 'I'll show you! With the £5 watch which I am selling for £2 I am going to give you not only a pair of carvers but, as a special advertisement, I am also going to give you half-a-dozen knives and forks.' We had all waited breathlessly to find out what more this wizard could produce, and when it came we were dumbfounded at first, and then there was a frantic rush of buyers.

My first inclination was to rush home for £2. I felt so helpless with only 4½d and such a tremendous bargain going. Charlie used the expression; 'Sold again and got the money', until the stock was exhausted.

When I got home and told my parents, they were not impressed. Perhaps the story was not so exciting at secondhand. Mother said the buyers may have got good value for money, but did they need either a watch or the cutlery? Two pounds to some of the buyers meant the best part of a year's wages.

When I left Charlie Lidget before lunch, the day had now cleared up, and I always remember what I thought was rather a sparkling answer by a young man to the usual query of a farmer: 'Do you want a place?' It was: 'Yes, to hang my coat.'

I did not spend any of my money until after I had made certain that my dinner was free. After that I made a tour of the shops to find out what was the best value for money. I decided not to patronise the big shops, but chose one that was rather out of the way, and in appearance very much like the one we had at home. I also noticed that it was kept by a rather homely woman.

I went in the shop to lay out my 4½d. I had never before had anything but a slate to write on, and I purchased a notebook, together with a special pencil, and an India rubber. This left me with 1d which I recklessly spent on sweets. Hitherto, I had never spent more than a ha'penny at a time. I was congratulated by the shopwoman on my wise spending, also by my parents later; and I eventually reached home with the inward glow of a day well spent.

7
CHURCH AND CHAPEL

> Such to this British Isle her Christian fanes,
> Each linked to each for kindred services;
> Her skies her steeple-towers with glittering vanes
> Far kenned, her chapels lurking among trees,
> Where a few villagers on bended knees
> Find solace which a busy world disdains.
>
> WORDSWORTH

My parents were big chapel people. We had no pictures in the house, but we had texts. The one at the head of my bed said: 'Be sure your sins will find you out.' The one at the foot said: 'My Grace is sufficient for thee.' Those whom my mother called 'the bettermos' sort of people' went to church. Our sort of people went to chapel.

In the three villages in our district which neighboured the halls of landed gentry there were churches but no chapels. Digby, however, had a manor house, not a hall, which made us rather superior to the poorer villages, and therefore we had a Wesleyan chapel as well as a church. Villages with neither Hall nor manor house were considered lower still in the social scale and had only a Primitive Methodist or even a Reform church.

In those days 90 per cent of the population went somewhere to worship, and we children certainly had our fair share of religious instruction. In the first place we attended a church school, where we started every day with a scripture lesson, learning catechisms, psalms and hymns parrot-fashion. This, however, was an everyday affair and had no effect on the emotions. Sundays at chapel were different.

There we started the day with Sunday-school in the mornings. The main theme was the after-life, and the prospects of going to

Heaven if you were good and to Hell if you were not. There was a fire-and-brimstone flavour about the teaching on the one hand, and, on the other, the picture of even Heaven itself was not attractive to children who were having a healthy and enjoyable time on earth.

Death seemed to permeate all forms of worship, particularly the hymns, and even the pleasant ones were about angels above the bright blue sky. One children's hymn that always made me feel depressed began:

> 'I would like to die,' said Willie
> 'If my papa could die too:
> But he says he isn't ready,
> 'Cos he's got so much to do.'

We also attended two chapel services later in the day. For children these were boring at best. The sermons meant little to us, and what they did mean was neither happy nor pleasant. Our preoccupation was to watch the big clock in the centre of the chapel. At the evening service I used to let my mind dwell pleasantly on what would be happening in a quarter of an hour after we had left chapel, when we should be sitting down to cold ham and hot vegetables, which had been put in the oven to warm up before we left home. Occasionally we stayed on for the prayer meeting after the evening service. This gave the members of the congregation an opportunity to express their religious emotions in a public way.

It was normally led by a man with a ready flow of evangelist fervour, followed by the less articulate brethren, whose halting sentences were intermingled with shouts of 'Praise the Lord!' and 'Hallelujah!' If there was a lull other members were called to witness by singing:

> Oh brother have you told how the Lord forgave?
> Let us hear you tell it over once again.

At the bottom of the aisle on either side the best people sat. These were the only pews having cushions. On the right were the

Misses Barlow, the grocers. On the left sat Mr William Bell, a farmer. He was the only man who came to chapel in a frock coat and top hat, except for one notable occasion.

In all the pews there were six seats, and in the bottom ones the charge was 10d a quarter for each person. All the others were 6d, except the one opposite the top pew. This was reserved for servant men who lived in at the farms nearby.

The only time I remember mother over-reaching herself was when they were getting on in the world. Mother thought that father ought to have a frock coat and a top hat, which he did get, much against his will. Apart from Aunt Emma's wedding, the first and only time he wore it was at the Sunday-school anniversary and he was obviously most uncomforable and embarrassed. It was one of the few times I knew him to put his foot down, but he refused to wear it ever afterwards. It was obvious that the wide gulf between the first pew and the bottom one could not be bridged by a frock coat and top hat.

My family were in the top pew, immediately behind the free seats, which were occupied by agricultural labourers, apprentices and visitors who were not guests of any of the pew occupants. The choir was more catholic in its composition and included a mixture from all classes. In the back row were the young men, the basses and the tenors, then came the young women, the contraltos and sopranos, and then two rows of children including myself.

We were always much interested to see the Preachers' Plan, which arrived each quarter and told us who our preachers would be for the next three months. They were chosen according to a complicated travel system, which started with a preacher who sometimes owned his own trap. He would collect and deposit preachers at each village as he went along to his own destination. As a result it invariably happened that our preachers came from within a radius of six miles. Some of them had been doing the same round for twenty or thirty years, and we knew all their idiosyncracies and most of their sermons by heart.

The most musical event that took place in my childhood was 'The Competition'. It was a singing contest among three neighbouring village choirs – Digby, Metheringham and Billinghay. Billinghay was the largest, had the most talent and was favourite from the start.

We travelled to the other two villages for this competition in the one-horse van owned by John Veal, the local carrier. The only really trained singer that we had in the choir was a newcomer to the village. She sang '*Ora pro nobis*' in a lush contralto and on all occasions got full marks. It was noticeable that, however cold the journey, she always travelled in front with Veal, who was a bachelor. Unfortunately, the competition did not last long enough for the romance to ripen.

It was our local celebrity, William Rooke, who wrote a poem for the competition which appeared in the local paper. I remember it started:

> As you go past our Chapel door,
>   You oft hear our musician,
> You say 'What's up?' – 'Why don't you know?
>   We're in for the Competition!'

Excitement became feverish when Digby's turn came to hold the competition. Never had so many people occupied the chapel at the same time. I can remember the moisture streaming down the walls. We lost, and the tragedy for me was that, at the knife-and-fork tea held afterwards, I accidentally overheard the tenor saying to somebody: 'Of course Fred Gresswell lost us the competition.' I was so dumbfounded that I burst into tears.

It appears that my voice had broken, so that when I was supposed to be singing treble, I was actually singing something between treble and bass. For years this preyed on my mind, and it was not until I was living in Keighley long after that the weight was lifted. One day I went into the public library and in a periodical in the reading room read some verses describing a similar tragedy that had been turned into a comedy. The lines remained in my mind and have given me ever since a memory as pleasant as the earlier experience was miserable. The piece is rather long to quote in full, but the first part will convey the idea:

When as a boy I sat the student's stool
I was an alto. (Altos as a rule
Are not abundant in a public school)
I was a wonder even then; folk
Thrilled when I sang, and marvelled when I spoke;
And then, oh horror! then it went and broke.
Stunned by the shock and muted for a space,
I held my peace, then blossomed forth a bass
Singing the treble when I lost my place . . .

The chapel choir provided the setting for many village romances and, during my time, there took place a romantic elopement which rent the social fabric of the congregation in two and sent our most distinguished chapel attender to church.

The chief tenor was a handsome young cousin of mine; he was an engine driver. The soprano was a very beautiful girl, the daughter of the farmer who sat in the back pew. It was well known that these two were in love and that the farmer opposed the match. We also knew that they met in secret at the Green Dykes on Sundays. One particular Sunday I was confidentially told that they were going to elope to Canada after the service. This was the most thrilling news I had ever received, and the air was electric. Most vividly I can remember staring at those two members who sang for what they knew was the last time in the chapel, and watching the hard-faced father who knew nothing about the plot.

Everything went according to plan, and that night they left the village. The girl was not even able to take any luggage with her. It was a nine days' wonder, and the chapel saw the farmer no more. After forty years of happy married life in Canada, my cousin's wife died and he returned to this country.

Just before that exciting elopement took place we had an evangelistic mission in the village. This was a great success, and the missioner, who came from Manchester, claimed that only one possible convert remained outside the fold. He was a signalman who had resisted on previous occasions. Though a good-living man, he refused to give a clean bill to the village, despite the entreaties of his wife and family and the whole of the chapel. Two friends and myself in the choir were among the last to succumb and it was a song from the Moody and Sankey Hymn Book which ultimately brought us to our knees on the penitent form:

Tell Mother I'll be There

The other day a message came and bade me quickly go,
If I would see my mother ere the Saviour took her home.
I promised her, before she died,
To Heaven I would repair,
Oh, Saviour, tell my mother, I'll be there.
Tell mother I'll be there,
In answer to her prayer,
Oh, tell my darling mother, I'll be there!

After the mission service we had a meeting at our house, and as the missioner was leaving next day, mother presented him with most of our treasured pig cheer – pork pies, potted meat, and other things of that sort. I was rather shocked to find that he had a home, wife and family on earth. I had been so used to hearing him describe his heavenly home.

To celebrate this outpouring of the spirit, mother decided to raise £70 to buy hundred-candle-power oil lamps for the chapel.

This was a very ambitious aim, but it was eventually achieved, though not without great effort and sacrifice by all the congregation. The idea was to build up the total by paying 1d a week each, by coffee suppers, sewing meetings and, as the culminating effort, a grand bazaar. My contribution was to make a hearthrug, which was almost certainly the most deplorable exhibit. I liked the coffee suppers, although at 4d I did not consider them value for the money.

Elementary education weakened the hold of evangelism over children of my generation. Though we had been 'converted', we soon found that not only did this form of worship mean nothing to us, but that we were no worse if we did without it. In other words, day-school teaching gave us a code of conduct which superseded the purely emotional influence of the chapel. Moreover, the local preachers were on the whole uneducated and had no power of reasoning which could appeal to children who had had some systematic instruction.

8
FEASTS AND FASTS

> Low lies that house where nut-brown draughts inspired,
> Where grey-beard mirth and smiling toil retired,
> Where village statesmen talk'd with looks profound,
> And news much older than their ale went round.
> Imagination fondly stoops to trace
> The parlour splendours of that festive place
>
> GOLDSMITH

Society was divided in our small community, even in the village pub, the Red Lion, which was the centre of social life for everything except religious functions. It had a large club room holding up to 100 people, and there parish meetings, property sales and all the club suppers took place. Of course, there were the two rooms in which drink was served.

The upper stratum – the farmers, shopkeepers and the shooting fraternity, which included the gamekeeper and gun-loaders – went into the bar parlour. Here they drank spirits or bottled beer, but, if their social status was unassailable, they could order draught beer too. They entered by a side door and could not be seen by the lower orders in the tap-room – the beaters, the rabbiters and the ratters, who were served through a hatch and sat on high wooden-backed seats. In the tap-room the usual request was for a quart, which, if I remember rightly, cost 4d at that time.

It was only at the week-end that the publican could afford two fires; for the rest of the week there was only one, in the tap-room. If it was very cold, the bar customers swallowed their pride and came to sit by it. One night a man of the village who was suspected of poaching came into the tap-room with his dog and gun and a well-filled game bag. He found sitting there the gamekeeper and the policeman, who would normally have been in the bar. At the sight of them he half-hesitated, then came in, put his bag down and called for his quart.

He took his seat amid a marked silence. The shoemaker, who was also a gun-loader, cleared his throat and enquired: 'Been shootin', like, a bit, mate?'

The poacher took his time before replying: 'Aye, mate, nobbit sparrers.'

Another pause and then: 'I was comin' past Bell's Buildings, and I see a cletch o'them between the stacks. I got down and had a shot. But when I went across to collect them there was not a single sparrer. There was a scuttleful o' legs. I was just that leg too low!'

The tension was relieved. He had offered an explanation. Nobody was compelled to challenge it.

It was usual for a boy to be allowed to go to the Red Lion on a Saturday night as soon as he started earning money. This was the high night of the week, when everybody would turn up and discuss the crops, the weather, social titbits and, of course, shooting.

I remember the first time I took the plunge and entered the bar. I was with a cousin; we were both about sixteen. He was a foundry worker, and I was a grocer's improver. Neither of our parents went to the pub and it was a fine point whether either of us was qualified to join the select company in the bar parlour. However, we boldly ordered two bottled beers and, after a tense moment whilst the landlord summed us up, were duly served. When the friendly voice of the gamekeeper enquired, 'And where may yar be working now mate?' we knew that we were accepted.

Although large quantities of beer were consumed, it was rarely that anyone got drunk. I saw only one drunken brawl, and that was at Feast time and the men concerned were from a neighbouring village. Beer was the natural drink at all times, and the beer allowance was the important factor in fixing the farm service agreements. Farmers usually stocked 36gal casks in harvest time for their workers, particularly thirsty Irishmen who came over in large numbers at that time of the year. Although my parents themselves were abstainers, they always bought a modest 9gal cask at haytime.

Tied farm servants, who received their beer allowance at their respective farms, rarely came to the public house except in May week, when, after paying their yearly bills, they often spent all their surplus money either on beer or at the local fairs.

It was in one of these young men that I first noticed a symptom of the great social change which was taking place. A boy who came from a large, hard-drinking family, and who had left school a year or two before, entered the school playground when he had received his May wages and showed us eight golden sovereigns. With these he said he was going to start a bank book; instead of the usual bottle of beer, he had with him a bottle of ginger pop.

We could not understand this because he had neither been 'saved', not had he joined the Band of Hope – previously the only reasons for not drinking. He said he had actually thought it out in his own head. His brothers worked all the year, then spent all they earned in one week's drinking. He had worked it out on paper that by doing without beer during May week he would have saved £100 by the time he was twenty-one. This sounded to us a colossal sum, but I heard later that he achieved his ambition.

There is no doubt that elementary education had been responsible for the difference between himself and his brothers. Children started thinking for themselves and having interests outside the narrow village circle.

There were two great days in the village year. One was the Feast Day, which occurred on the first Sunday after 19 July. On the following Tuesday there were village sports, for which everybody had a half-day off. In my childhood we looked forward to this time because a small fair came to the village. It consisted of a little roundabout and a stall at which gaudy objects were sold. In the sports the children would run races for sixpences, which would quickly be spent at the fair.

This very special holiday is maintained in our village to this day and in most of the villages of the district, although the old type of fair has disappeared. It is a time of reunion for the villagers. Friends and relations come from far and near to spend the day together. I still attend these gatherings.

The other important day – not now observed – was called

Leaving Day. It mainly concerned the single men in service on the farm and the domestic girl workers. In a way there were two 'leaving days'. The married families always moved to a job on 6 April, and not on any other day. The young people's Leaving Day was 15 May. On that May morning all the married people would have been installed, and were prepared to take charge for the week while the young people would be away.

The living-in farm servants of both sexes drew their money in golden sovereigns on 15 May. They then trooped down to the village to pay the year's accounts with the tailor and the shoemaker. It was customary to have one pair of new hand-made boots every three years, costing 30s. Suits, which were bought less frequently, were priced at from £2 to £3. On settling day the tailor and shoemaker always provided a dish of stuffed chine for their customers.

The Monday after 15 May was a big day for these young people. It was the May Fair in the town of Sleaford. While they enjoyed the fun of the fair, they had the thrill of being hired by a new employer if they were not 'staying on'. In the streets there was only one question: 'Have you got a place?'

The wages paid in my boyhood amounted to £3 a year on leaving school for girls, and £5 for boys. The second year, £5 and £8 respectively. The third year the sum was £16 for boys,who in that third year were known as 'seconds' – that is, second to the wagoner. After that they were usually full-blown wagoners, rising from £20 to £26 on a twelve-horse farm and upwards. Girls earned up to £20 a year. When my mother started work at the age of twelve, she received 10s from Christmas to May, with the material for a print frock, and the next year 30s for the full year, with material for an afternoon dress.

Living conditions on the farms varied greatly, but the best type of farmer used to boast of providing seven meals a day, four of which were based on bacon. It was usual for serving men who lived in to get up at half-past four in the morning to groom the horses, and these started work at six o'clock. On rising the men got the 'dew bit', probably tea and bread and butter. Before they went to work with the horses they had breakfast. At nine o'clock they had lunch in the fields – a large chunk of bread and fat bacon. Then they went through until they brought the horses in at half-past two, when they had dinner. At six-thirty they had supper, and at nine o'clock a 'bed bit' – which might be milk with bread and butter.

The main advantage of living in the country was that everybody had a garden. In my young days we were nearly self-supporting, and many a time our grocery order for the week consisted of tea and sugar only.

Every cottage labourer had one pig or more. They were his most important possessions, and he depended on them for his supply of meat during the year. As I have explained, pigs were always a big topic of conversation in the village, and after the usual greeting it was quite normal to ask how the pigs were doing. My people never got out of this habit, and in later years, when I visited my home, mother would invariably ask: 'Have you been to see the pigs?'

After a pig in the district had been killed the important thing was to buy one to feed for next year, and there was much talk and speculation when a sow had farrowed a litter. The piglets would be furtively looked at during the first few weeks after birth, for they were not marketable until they were eight weeks old. By that time, if the litter was any good, the pigs were spoken for by one or another. But sometimes people bought a pig in a poke, like one man who agreed to take two unseen. When the farmer came out the prospective buyer said: 'I'll hev that for one.' He picked out the best. The farmer said, 'Catch it', and it was caught and bagged.

'I'll hev that for another', says Sam. 'Oh no you won't', says the farmer. 'You've had your pick, and now it's my turn.' The farmer chose the smallest. Sam said: 'How much are they?' and the farmer replied: 'Thirty shillings each.' At this Sam turned pale, but added: 'I'll be a man of my word.'

Sam's wife looked at the pigs and started to weep. 'You can take them back, I won't have them', she said. In the end, however, she accepted them. She was a good pig-feeder and nursed them carefully and got them to a good size.

Such was the importance of pigs in a village life that they were placed on a par with sermons. A man was heard to remark to the local preacher on leaving chapel: 'By goy, boy, but you did preach a good sermon, mate! By goy, but I have got a good pig in my sty!'

The most important club in the village was the Pig Club, and my father was its secretary for more than thirty years. The subscription was 6d a month per pig. In the case of illness the secretary was immediately notified, and a committee of inspection was sent. They would decide if the pig had to be destroyed and whether anything could be salvaged. On an average, not more than one or two died in a year, and we never had a major catasttophe like foot-and-mouth disease, which would have swamped the funds. After fifty years the Club had accumulated £90.

It gave an annual supper except when there had been an extra drain on the funds. This was the big social event at the inn, and everybody would go through his own particular repertory of songs. There were four courses to the meal: beef, mutton, pork and plum pudding. The hearty eaters sampled each dish in turn, to see which they liked best. Having decided this, they would really settle down to it. I had my first half-pint of beer at one of these suppers, but the normal helping was a quart.

The great stand-by throughout the winter for luxury food was what we knew as pig-cheer. From the beginning to the end of winter the villagers killed their pigs one after the other. The family groups provided each other in turn with this pig-cheer.

For instance, when we killed our pig, which was around 36 stone, on the first day there would be pig's fry, which consisted of sweetbread, liver and bits of pork. This would be sent round to our particular relatives and friends, who would repay the compliment in due course. Then my mother would make anything from nine to twelve pork pies, strings of sausages (fifty to sixty sausages in all) and what is known as collared rind, which was rather gristly but had a good taste. She would also make bone-pies and hazlitt (haslet) – a sort of potted meat.

But the choicest dish was pork pie. These pies weighed 3lb or 4lb each and would keep, although we would usually give away three or four to special friends. With the addition of exchange gifts, we could be certain of pork pies every Sunday for three months. We had two boiled sausages each for tea every Saturday night all through the winter, with lashings of toast and gravy.

It could be said that, apart from bread, bacon was the staple food of the village throughout the year – usually cold bacon for breakfast and every midday meal, and hot bacon at night. On Sunday morning it would be fried bacon. A variation would be stuffed chine in May. This was bacon stuffed with every type of herb that grows in the spring, such as nettles, marjoram, thyme and even rose leaves. The ordinary farm labourer's midday dinner in the fields consisted of one piece of bread with thick fat bacon.

We could have as many eggs as we wanted when there were more than eighteen to the shilling. This happened for about one month in the year, around Easter time. We had fresh meat only about twice a year in my early days – at Christmas and at one of the village feasts. Later on we had fresh meat about once a month. Occasionally mutton appeared unexpectedly, when what is known in the country as 'killing a dead sheep' occurred. If a sheep had to be killed because of accidental injury, for example, it was sold cheaply to the villagers by the farmer. In harvest time, of course, we had a plethora of rabbits.

Churning butter was done on Monday nights in winter, and between four and five o'clock on Tuesday mornings in summer. While making butter may sound a very pleasant job, there were a lot of preliminaries before the milk reached the final stage. However small and poor the farmstead, there was usually a cool dairy. We had both a good dairy and pantry although they were attached to a small-holding of 3 acres. We had not a great deal of cream for butter, for most of our milk was sold in the village, but the labour involved in making our small quantity of about 10lb was the same as in making 50lb.

The dairy was lined with tiers of stone slabs. One level had new milk, another day-old milk, and the other two-day-old milk. The milk was placed in what we called pancheons; those wide shallow bowls helped the cream to settle on top. Every day the milk was 'siled'. (This may be a Lincolnshire word for a tinned slicer something like a thin sieve, with which the cream was skimmed off.) After the first day's cream had been taken off, what was left could be sold as skimmed milk. I think this fetched about 4d per gallon. We used to call this 'blue' milk. The cream was regularly skimmed off for three days and the surplus milk put in the pig swill.

Churning cream into butter could be a very tedious and exasperating business, but perhaps I only remember the worst occasion. Normally the operation would take about twenty minutes in summer and half an hour or more in winter. The churn was an oblong barrel turned by a handle. This needed a steady rhythm, not too quick or too slow, otherwise something happened that stopped the cream from turning. The common expression was that it 'went to sleep'.

If it went to sleep when I was churning I was blamed for turning too quickly or too slowly, but if my mother was in the same predicament she claimed it was the weather. If there was no sign of butter in half an hour it was sure to be a long-drawn-out process, which could go on for hours. To try and 'wake' it up, hot water would be put in the churn occasionally, and all the family would have a go at the handle.

The pride of every farm wife was the quality of saleability of her butter, and when patting it up into half-pounds and pounds, she always finished by putting on top her own particular hallmark. In buying butter from the local grocer's people always knew whose it was; they could tell by the mark. Some farm wives added artificial colouring to the cream. They also introduced ingredients to take away the strong taste when the cows had been eating too many buttercups in high summer or, what was worse, to camouflage the effects of dirty cow-houses and utensils. You could always tell by the butter whether it came from a clean farmhouse or not.

Country life has its joys, but there are always unforseen hazards. When I am in tropical countries I always look out for snakes in the grass. In England one never expects worse than rabbit holes, yet one summer's day, quite one of the blue, I was involved in a painful affair. I was going up to Ashby to fetch the cows when a town boy who was staying at the policeman's said he would like to go with me. Passing a small field called the Penfold, we stood and watched a man with two horses reaping the grass. This small croft was once used as a pound for stray cattle. It was very little used at that time and was full of weeds and nettles.

All at once as we watched, the horses reared and plunged, broke away from the reaper and raced madly towards us. We jumped out of the way and saw that the man who had been riding on the reaper was rolling in agony on the ground. At the same time we were surrounded by a swarm of wasps. The boy who was with me ran away yelling at the top of his voice; he had been very badly stung. Strangely enough, although I was fighting the wasps off too, I was not stung and have never been stung since. The boy and the man were both ill for weeks afterwards.

9
COUNTRY CHARACTERS

> Happy the man who far from schemes of business, like the early generations of mankind, ploughs and ploughs again his ancestral land with oxen of his own breeding, with no yoke of usary on his neck!
>
> HORACE

The most versatile man in the village was William Rooke, carpenter, joiner and undertaker. He was a patriarchal character with a flowing beard, and besides being the most noted local preacher, he was a philosopher and a poet, and on occasion provided a not unacceptable bass in the chapel choir. What was more important to me, he was a boy's man. I have never forgotten how I went down the street with him one day, expressing my views on a certain subject, and how he turned round on me and said: 'God bless my life and soul, boy! You don't mean to tell me you think that!' He was the only man I knew who allowed me to argue with him.

The Rookes, a large family, lived next door to the chapel (their grandson still lives there) and they used to entertain most of the local preachers on Sunday. Our family was also on visiting terms, and it was the highlight of the week to go to the Rookes for an hour on Sunday night.

I vividly remember those Sunday evenings. We were entertained in a large, cosy room, the supper things often still on the table, and the local preacher still there waiting to be collected. They always had the same meal every Sunday – a large joint of beef and cold potatoes. The rest of the village we 'neighboured' – that is to say, we were friendly with them, but did not visit them.

William Rooke and his wife both suffered from ill-health. I remember on one occasion I was driving Mr Rooke to a preaching appointment in a village four miles away. He was just recovering from a severe attack of bronchitis. We got half way to our destination, when he complained of feeling cold. All at once he pulled the pony up, felt inside his coat, and said: 'Good God, boy! 'I've forgotten to put on my undershirt!' Young as I was, I realised that this might prove disastrous, and I suggested turning back. He said, 'No, I'll say a prayer', which he did; and we then proceeded. All of us in the family were concerned for the next few days about him, but later he told me that his prayer had been answered and that he had suffered no ill effects.

William Rooke was a man indifferent to money matters and, through poor health and the long credits he was obliged to give, he was hard up. When the butcher's cart came round on a Saturday, those who could indulge in fresh meat chose their frugal joint carefully, but not William Rooke, who had no small or niggardly mind. He would not bargain with the butcher for something cheap, but in the grand manner would produce half-a-crown and say: 'I have a wife and seven children, and I am expecting the parson on Sunday. Do the best you can with this.' He always managed to get the choicest joints.

It was always an anxious time when his traveller was expected. (Most of the village tradesmen dealt with one wholesale firm who sent a traveller periodically to collect the accounts and take new orders.) People would peep behind the curtain and say: 'His traveller has come.' Mother would then invariably get a note asking if we had anything in the house that could be borrowed temporarily. As father was treasurer of the Pig Club, it was well known that we had to keep £5 in the house for emergency claims. This money was usually lent to help Rooke.

On only one occasion was the request for some reason refused, and it so happened that on the next Sunday Mr Rooke was preaching at our chapel. I cannot remember his text, but the general subject was 'the tragedy of the pocket', and he made a scathing attack on people who 'hoarded' money. He even went so far as to say that more evil was created through saving than by 'the barrel', and that the ignorance and selfishness of miserly people was keeping back the world's progress. This reference to the barrel' shocked the Band of Hope camp, of which my people vere ardent members.

The congregation, of course, knew the real reason for the outburst and no doubt agreed that the rebuke was merited. It was generally thought that my parents, who had risen in a few years rom nothing to owning a small dairy farm, were becoming too noney-conscious. As a result of this sermon the two families – the Rookes and the Gresswells – were not on speaking terms for a vhile. But there is always somebody either dying or getting narried, and such events in a village automatically bring people ogether.

One woman in our village had a crow for a pet. Mr Rooke stopped one day to look at it and remarked: 'I've reared a lot of ooks in my time, but I've never tamed one.' He certainly had a arge family. One of his children spent so much time with the illage postman, Thomas Rawdon, and his childless wife, that hey arranged to adopt him. He was a bright lad and eventually became a clergyman.

Thomas Rawdon was another village character. He was a natural handyman, the sort of person who, when everyone else vas at work, would always be on the spot in an emergency. Apart from his Post Office duties, he was the local sexton, bell-inger, overseer for the poor and parish clerk. He was such an ll-round man that, in addition to his manifold church duties, he etained his ticket of chapel membership and attended his class egularly on Wednesday night.

Rawdon was also responsible for ringing all the pigs in the illage and eventually killing them. During the winter months, his time was mostly occupied with this task, and the squeals of lying pigs echoed round the village. Normally he would kill only one a day. In the morning he would cut its throat, scrape it nd hang it up. In the evening he would come round, cut it up and alt it. For this he would charge 1s 6d a day and his claim was that, fter he had cut a pig up, you could use everything but the squeal.

Another of the village's odd personalities was a man named Arthur. I never knew his surname, if he had one. He was the ag-and-bone merchant. He was a quiet, unassuming man who

had something the matter with one leg and walked with a crutch
His business depended mainly on exchanging rabbit skins an
any old clothes or bones for his miscellaneous stock of smallware
Arthur would call perhaps once a month, and he had a rathe
simple but effective method of salesmanship. He went round wit
a small pony and trap, the harness of which was held togethe
mainly by string. With his crutch under one arm, and the hug
basket containing his stock-in-trade in the other, he struggle
slowly to the door of each house, and when he had put his baske
down it would be a few minutes before he could get his breath t
take it back again.

He was also something in the nature of a quack doctor; i
there was no deal to be made he would pass the time discussin
the ailments in the family. Meanwhile, the contents of the baske
looked bright and cheerful. Overflowing its sides were laces fo
children and grown-ups, brown and black and of all sizes an
thicknesses. In the centre would be cheap watches and clocks
These articles were more in the nature of a shop window display
and I never saw anybody buy them. The main stock was for mor
everyday use – small oddments such as buttons, tapes, threads
studs, and penny packets of notepaper and envelopes.

While I used to trade with him regularly, I was not one o
Arthur's best cutomers; my transactions were too one-sided.
always wanted cash and therefore was not able to make quite such
a good bargain as the people who would take something i
exchange. If possible, of course, he preferred to give a service
such as advice on ailments, and only on one occasion did I fall fo
this. Like most children in the country I was troubled with wart
on my hands, and Arthur had a reputation for being able to cur
them by some sort of magic. So once when I brought him
rabbit skin that was worth, say 1d, I asked him if he could cur
the warts instead of giving me the money.

He said he usually charged 3d but as I was a valued custome
he would make an exception. He asked to have a look at th
warts, which I showed him, and then to my surprise he suggeste
no treatment. In fact, I cannot remember him touching them
but he said they would be gone in a week. When I asked him if h

vas not going to do anything else he said 'no'. I thought at the ime, of course, that the whole thing was a fake, but I was urprised when they actually did disappear within the time. I don't now the answer to this day. My sister has since told me that she ad her warts cured by Arthur for a ha'penny. Perhaps I wasn't o shrewd after all.

We all knew each other intimately, and it was customary to pass he time of day when meeting anyone in the village. Sometimes he adults were not on speaking terms and passed each other in tony silence, but all the children would exchange greetings vhenever they met.

Mrs Lacey, who was looked upon as a witch, always replied to Good morning' by saying: 'Yes, lovey'. Joe Gill would perhaps top and look at the sky and say 'Mebbe it is', or 'You think so lo you?'

This was an unusual character. He was a thick-set man with a ushy beard. He lived with his wife and family in a very pleasant ottage in the centre of the village. In his youth he had emigrated o Canada and had been a lumberjack in the backwoods there. Having inherited a small farm together with a cottage at Digby, ie came home to a semi-independent existence. Machinery was iis passion, and while he had no regular employment, in anything o do with machinery or felling trees he was in great demand. He vas an excellent worker at any job he undertook, but did not take n any more than was absolutely necessary; therefore his inde-endence was not extended to his wife and family. His children vent to the village school, and the boys went into some sort of rade, but the girls had to be content with better-class domestic ervice.

He was a man of moods, and sometimes he would make friendly onversation with the children of the village; on other occasions ie could be very severe. I remember being with his son and two or hree other boys, sitting on top of the farmyard gate. He came up n what appeared to be a friendly way, and then said: 'I have told ou once about sitting on the gate. I have told you twice. The hird time I will sweep the gate with my strap.' We had not ioticed that whilst he was talking he was unbuckling his belt, and, sure enough, each one of us got a lusty whack with it.

Joe Gill was a crony of William Rooke, the carpenter, and was always called in to help when there was any wood sawing to do. On one occasion they were working in a field, and Joe had already got there and set the bench in position for the wood to be hauled up when William arrived. He said: 'You cap me, Joe, putting that bench there. You should have known better.' Joe replied, 'Oh you are that side out are you, William! In that case I bid you good morning', and off he went. When I witnessed this I thought it was the end of a long partnership, but in passing the carpenter's shop in the afternoon I saw them laughing and talking together as though nothing had happened. It was said that Joe could move as much timber as two or three men put together, and if a tree was cut he could put a stake in the exact position it would fall. After harvest he went round the countryside with my cousin's threshing machine.

It was the custom of the farmers to provide meals for the machine-men, and they vied with each other in putting on a good table. I overheard my cousin telling someone: 'I was thoroughly ashamed of my mate, Joe, today. He let us down badly. We were threshing at Mrs Leedale's, and when we went into breakfast there was a whole ham on the table, a leg of mutton and a big piece of beef. Joe had a plateful of ham, and was looking round the table, when Mrs Leedale said, "Can you eat an egg?", Joe replied, "I once knew a man who ate two."'

Anyway he was well known for his idiosyncrasies, and it was all taken in good part, but he could not stand being patronised.

The Gills were a musical family and were the proud possessors of an organ. His wife was a regular chapel-goer. I used to go to the musical evenings, not only as a boy, but also whenever I was at home as a young man. The father never joined in, and as we passed through the kitchen he was usually sitting with his feet up on the mantelpiece, reading. Sometimes he greeted us, but he invariably shouted some caustic comment on the performance. He had a good voice himself, and at the Pig Club suppers, etc., he used to sing a song:

First apprenticeship: the author, aged thirteen, as a grocer's assistant *(right)*

The Gresswells' first trip abroad: the author with May in Menton in 1924

Three golfing sisters (the firm of Baxandalls): Emily, Annie and May (Mrs Fred Gresswell) in 1945

The author's wife, May, with a golfing trophy

So what is the use of repining!
 Where there's a will there's a way,
Tomorrow the sun will be shining,
 Although it looks cloudy today.

Joe was not an intellectual, but, through his colonial experiences, he had acquired some measure of culture. He was better dressed than most people in the village, and raised his hat, shook hands, and talked like a gentleman. Normally people in the village did not shake hands. I was thirteen years old when I had to shake hands for the first time, and I remember being very self-conscious about it. I was in fact eighteen before I realised that one should grip the hand instead of giving a limp touch.

The village hen-huckster was an irascible Irishman called McCann. Although he lived in the village most of his life, he never 'belonged', and had to depend for his living on poultry dealing outside Digby. He had a high trap and sat on top of cages full of birds which squawked through the village when he came home at night. Several of his family went to school with me. Only one of them tried to work on the land, and he ran away after a week because he said they had tried to feed him with 'run-up-the-tree', which was our phrase for foreign bacon. This was considered a lame excuse, for the normal reason for running away was not getting sufficient to eat.

It was certainly an experience to visit McCann's pulling pens a week or two before Christmas. All his large family worked day and night plucking birds. The killing of these was merely incidental. It required a quick screw of the neck, and by that time half the feathers would be off. The McCann's always worked waist deep in feathers, down and lice.

The Browns, mentioned previously as one of the three main families in the village, were semi-tradespeople. One brother, Sumner, was a tailor. Unfortunately, he did not have the use of his legs and went about on crutches. In spite of his disability, however, he was able to take an interest in everything that went on in the village, because his shop had windows on two sides, overlooking the school, the public house, the saddler's and the grocer's. Moreover, everyone in the village had to pass him to get to the post office, which was next door to his shop.

It was remarkable to see the way he got about from counter to counter with or without crutches. Unaided he could get the cloth down from his shelves, measure, and fit his customers. In his side window he had the only men's outfitting display in the village. It usually consisted of some studs, a cap and a tie. Because of its position, Sumner's shop was the centre of village gossip.

Sumner's sister was the Miss Biddy Brown who paid me ½d a week for doing her shopping. She was the village dressmaker. Another brother, Charlie, was agent for a firm of coal merchants and occupied a cosy hut at the railway station, where he took orders. He was excluded from the full status of tradesman because he had to help unload coal from the railway wagons, although in no circumstances would he have delivered.

Charlie was the chairman of the bar at the Red Lion. He occupied the grandfather chair next to the fireplace and this had to be vacated immediately he came in at 7pm prompt. He left at nine o'clock, during which time he consumed two pints. He was a man of few words and, except regarding his chair, he never asserted his authority. I never heard him say anything noteworthy, but he was steady and reliable and always in his place at the appointed hour.

But for George Brown, the brother of these three, the Boer War might have passed unnoticed in the village. It certainly had the effect of transforming him overnight from a black sheep into a village hero.

This was a big, happy-go-lucky fellow who, not being fond of work, used to roam the district doing casual jobs. On one occasion it was rumoured that he had stayed several days at the Sleaford Union, a branch of the workhouse reserved for casuals. This scandal never came to light because of a difference between the two overseers of the parish – McCann, who wanted the matter ventilated, and Rooke, who was instrumental in having it hushed up. All was forgotten overnight when George Brown enlisted in the Army and volunteered for service in South Africa. In due course he arrived there, sole representative of his village. We on our part were very conscious of the honour and responsibility which had been thrust upon us. We were now personally represented, and it became Digby's war.

I remember the change taking place. From the moment of George Brown's arrival in South Africa everybody took a lively interest in the fighting, even the oldest inhabitant. He had lived through the Crimean War, and every time we talked about the enemy he used to say: 'What, our 'ands? What, the Rooshans?' Everything in the village was now on a war footing. The women had sewing meetings to make Army comforts. The children learned patriotic songs. At that time I had a schoolboy attraction for the village schoolmaster's daughter. Her name was Dolly Clow, and 'Goodbye, Dolly I must leave you', had an additional appeal for me. Children were christened with the names of war heroes and the chorus of a popular song went:

> The baby's name is Kitchener,
> Carrington, Methuen, Gatwick White,
> Cronje, Plumer, Majuba . . .

and so on.

We followed with keen interest the news of the famous sieges, and when word came through that Mafeking had been relieved there was great excitement. Later in the day, as I had to fetch the cows from Ashby, I thought it would be a good idea to take the glad tidings to this out-of-the-way village. I persuaded two of the boys to accompany me, and with some home-made flags we paraded the village street and shouted patriotic songs. The first man we encountered was the gardener from the Hall. Carried away by the excitement, he jumped off his bicycle and gave us 1d.

This suggested new possibilities to us. We immediately started a collection and accumulated the sum of 9d. Unfortunately, when we got back to Digby we found that the rumour of the relief of Mafeking was unfounded. This placed us in a difficult position, but we had not indicated that the money was going to any special cause, and we decided to divide the 9d between us. I remember that I had a slightly uneasy conscience in accepting my 3d and it was satisfied only when I convinced myself that it was impossible to return the money to the right people. I went so far as to make the pious decision that I would not touch the money until Mafeking had actually been relieved.

My heart missed a beat the next day because, while we were in school, a policeman came to the door and asked for me. What a relief it was to find that he was seeking my assistance! He had a gipsy with him whom he had caught red-handed stealing some chickens, and he was taking him to the lock-up at Sleaford seven miles away. Our pony and trap had been hired for the trip, and I was the only available driver. I felt important about being involved in this criminal affair, but I was also rather nervous of the gipsy and insisted on the policeman sitting between us.

The journey took an hour, and on our way the gipsy gave us his views on many things, including war. Country people, of course, always think gipsies possess supernatural powers, and when he told us that in his opinion the war would last another two years, I began to regret my decision to hold the money I had made till victory was won. About halfway to Sleaford, to my consternation, some gipsies appeared from the hedges and surrounded us. They ignored both the policeman and myself and talked to the prisoner in a language we could not understand. Eventually they handed over two gold sovereigns to our passenger, and we were allowed to go on.

Arriving in Sleaford, we stabled the pony and the policeman took the prisoner to the police station, telling me to wait outside a shop until he came back. It must then have been about twelve noon, and I was still waiting in exactly the same place at four o'clock in the afternoon. I can remember every detail of the contents of that shop window. I saw it again recently and, after eighty years I was almost sure some of the same things were still in it!

The gipsy's prophecy proved wrong, and Mafeking was relieved shortly afterwards. In due course we had the tremendous thrill of welcoming home the village hero, George Brown. Before he arrived there was much discussion as to how we should ceremonially honour the returned soldier. Eventually, through the influence of the station-master, a permanent job was found for him as a platelayer on the line.

I remember that we waited at the station for several trains before he eventually arrived. We marched in front of him back to his home, and while I do not think there was any speechmaking, we seemed to have had nothing else to do then but stand outside the cottage, waiting for him to reappear. This he did in due course in order to go to the Red Lion, where he celebrated for the rest of the evening. There he regaled the company with stories of armoured trains on the wild karoo and the dangers of the rolling veld. He said that what had buoyed him up and sustained him through all the dangers of battle and siege were the memorable words of his mother, who said to him before he left: 'You'll be alreet. Them as is nowt never 'appens owt.'

Mother delivered letters to the village of Rowston, a mile from Digby, and there were plenty of 'characters' in that direction. The village was almost in a *cul de sac*; the only proper road was through Digby, although there was access by field roads and fording a stream in other directions. The village comprised the church, vicarage, manor house, Reform chapel, a small general store, a carpenter's shop, several small farms and some cottages. In 1821 the census showed a population of 125 persons, and it had probably not altered much by 1900.

The villagers were dependent on Digby for railway facilities, also for the public house and post office and all the trades, except the carpenter. Although its roots were as old as ours, Rowston was looked upon by Digby people as a poor relation with a slightly lower mentality. The farms were poor; one was known for its bad butter, and it was rumoured that this farm fed its pigs on fish meal.

My views may have been rather prejudiced because of what we thought was the main action of a farmer living in one of the outlying fen farms. There were several outlying places on the postal round. One of them, called Tally Ho, the birthplace of my mother, was a mile from the village across fields. To reach this place it was necessary to open gates and climb fences. Before mother went on her round she called at home, and if there was any open and non-urgent correspondence for this part, such as circulars, bills or postcards, she might hold them another day until something more important came. This was by arrangement with all the people concerned, except Freeman Love, who had a fair-sized farm at the very farthest point, about a mile down a dirt-track road. He not only insisted on everything being delivered each day, but made certain by ordering a ½d daily paper to be sent by post every morning. The only time I knew mother to refuse a Christmas box was when he offered her 1s. There was no love lost between them.

There were two outstanding characters in Rowston. Copen was a shopkeeper who achieved independence through his enterprise; he was ultimately responsible for building the Reform chapel. When the railway was being built a navvy came into his shop and said: 'Can you trust me for a half-ounce of thick twist until pay day?' 'No', said Mr Copen, 'but I will give you a half-ounce.' That started a big trade with railway workers. The news spread quickly. I thought it was most daring and enterprising to run the risk of actually giving something for nothing as advertisement.

Herbert Allan, the carpenter, was another well-known character. He had many quaint ways and a good knowledge of the Bible. He made his own coffin several years in advance and used it as a kitchen cupboard to keep tea and sugar in. He also made his brother's coffin. These two stood on end in the kitchen. His brother did not like the idea, and his coffin was eventually sold for someone else.

There were several hard drinkers in the village. I remember hearing a man say he would like to cut his throat to make it wider so that he could drink more beer.

Much amusement was caused by a story that went round that the fireirons in a certain farmhouse could not be found. The farmer employed a housekeeper and two maids. The housekeeper accused the housemaids. They said at first they did not know where the irons were, but at last she threatened to call in the police, so the maids told her that if she had slept in her own bed during the last week, she would have known where they were. The farmer married the housekeeper shortly afterwards.

Rowston also had a successful evangelistic revival. Most of the people were converted, and many were persuaded to sign the pledge, but it was found in spite of this that many single girls were expecting babies, and a meeting was called to see what could be done. Many people made suggestions, and then Mrs Piggot the village midwife was called in. She said: 'You can do all the converting you like, but you'll never convert 'em below the navel.'

I have hesitated to relate this story, but it is true, and there is a moral to it. Where religious teaching failed, apparently elementary education succeeded. There was a distinct fall in the birth of illegitimate children after a decade of compulsory education. In the 'eighties there were many single girls in the village, who either had children or had to get married, but among the girls who went to school in my time I do not know of one who got into what they called 'trouble'.

10
POWERS THAT WERE

> It is not now, as it hath been of yore: –
> Turn where so'er I may:
> By night or day,
> The things which I have seen, I can now see no more.
>
> WORDSWORTH

Our local characters had only local interest. We all knew them; they were our familiars. In my boyhood, however, our lives were governed by certain institutions, more remote and incalculable. Of these the gentry were perhaps the most important. They wielded an influence – and provided local employment – on a scale unthinkable today.

There were three Halls in the immediate vicinity. The most notable was Blankney. This was the country seat of the Rt Hon H. H. Chaplin. He was a member of the Government, but he was known locally simply as Squire Chaplin. The estate comprised most of the land in that district, and was reputed to have a rent roll of £60,000 per annum. It was said that he could ride seven miles on horseback through his own estate.

Blankney village was one of the pleasantest in our part of the world. It was mainly occupied by the staff and employees of the Hall and the home farm. It was also the headquarters of the Blankney Hunt. The Hall was separated from the main road by wide, sweeping lawns. It was an imposing residence and had been the scene of many historic gatherings. I have never been inside, but as a small boy of five or six I walked to Blankney – three miles – to a garden fête in the grounds. This event impressed itself on my mind because it was dark when we left and I got separated from my parents among what seemed to me to be a huge crowd of people. There were no lights of course; it was just a matter of standing and calling out. This was ineffective, and I felt very lost and forsaken. Eventually, somebody took me to the main gate and remained with me until my parents turned up after searching for me everywhere.

Squire Chaplin was the representative of the Grantham district, which comprised all our area, in Parliament. He was a popular and generous landlord. One of the stories that I remember hearing about him concerned a farmer who stopped him one day and asked him if he could make a reduction in his rent. The Squire replied: 'That means I have to pay you something. You haven't paid me a penny rent for years.'

Squire Chaplin's political mistake was that he took his constituency too much for granted. It was supposed to be a safe seat, and at election time he did not trouble to spend much time in the district. His organisation failed to notice that the ground was being cut from underneath his feet. A Professor Lupton, an engineer from Leeds, was the Liberal candidate. In the first place, nobody took much notice of him, but he had some progressive ideas. One which appealed very much to country people was an old-age pension. I can well remember my father saying that Chaplin had said that 5s a week old-age pension for everyone in England would ruin the country.

Lupton's methods of canvassing were very quiet, but penetrating. There was no such thing as a loud-speaker in those days, but if he was going to speak in the village in the evening, he and his daughter would go down every street on their bicycles, ringing a small handbell and saying: 'Have you heard about the meeting? Are you coming to the meeting?' While he had no mass demonstrations, Lupton's methods had the effect of making personal contact with practically everyone in the constituency and, to everyone's amazement, at the next election he won the day. Nobody was more surprised than Squire Chaplin, who, sometime afterwards, was promoted to the House of Lords. The estate passed to Lord Londesborough.

If we could have seen it, this was a sure sign that the Old Order was passing. Later on I shall describe some of the more recent changes in our village and the district, but the reader may be interested in the size of gentlemen's establishments in those spacious days. At Bloxholm Hall in 1897–8 there were employed one butler, one coachman, one stud groom, three footman and fourteen female servants. Ten grooms looked after fourteen hunters, one or two hacks and two carriage horses. A gentleman went hunting with two horses, a groom riding the spare behind him. And this vast establishment was considered necessary for a family of only two people.

We had our own order of precedence nearer home. There were Browns, and Browns of Digby. Actually, there were three families of that name, but each of a different species. First, there were the Digby Browns, then Brown the butcher, who came from Ruskington. There was nothing very noticeable about him, except that he was very typical of his own trade – a big, burly sort of man who, on Feast Days and special occasions, with a view to advertising his wares, exhibited the tying-up of a fat beast in front of his butcher's shop and felling it with a pole-axe. He delivered round the village in a high butcher's cart, and he always had a high-stepping horse to challenge any would-be racers on the road.

The Manor Browns were the aristocrats of the village. My first recollection of the manor house was that it was occupied most of the year by the farm bailiff, Mr Joe Ogden, who ran the farm for the absentee landlord. But two or three times a year, particularly in summer and usually for haytime and harvest, the owner and his family took up residence for a few weeks.

The manor house itself is peculiarly sited. The house is directly on the road, and the main rooms have French windows. This enabled curious people from the village almost to see what they were having for dinner. Directly opposite the house on the other side of the road were the gardens, lawns and tennis courts. At that time, these were beautifully kept, but whether the family were having tea on the lawn, or playing tennis, they were in the public eye. Only the walled-in vegetable garden was private. I suppose in the main the villagers were very discreet, and when they had to pass that way, averted their eyes.

I thought this was an ideal way of living, and it was always my ambition to farm in this style, a subject on which I shall have something to say later on. This went on for a few years, and then changes took place. I don't know why they left, unless the farm did not pay and had become too expensive for a holiday residence.

They were then followed by Mr and Mrs Pereira Brown (yet more Browns, but it was mere coincidence), who had recently married in early middle age. Mr Brown was a gentleman farmer, which in those days indicated that they had some outside investments that made them independent of farming alone. It was immediately recognised in the village that the Browns were a cut above the ordinary farmers, if not quite up to the County class. It was surprising the difference it made when the villagers had someone they could look up to. Pereira Brown had one disability. He stammered badly, but he was a man who could command respect in spite of his handicap. He not only became the leader of the village activities, but he was also a county councillor and a magistrate. His wife also took a leading part in the women's activities, and between them they set a good example to the village.

She, perhaps, carried it too far in that she endeavoured to keep the village free from all vice. Some years afterwards a noted author came to the next village. In the books he published about that time he brought in incidents about the hunting fraternity and the questionable morals of the County people. One of these books filtered into the small library in the village, and Mrs Brown immediately had it confiscated.

At this period, picture postcards made their appearance. The first ones I saw were photographs of Marie Studholme and Phyllis Dare. They cost 2d each and were exhibited in the small tailor's shop window. They were the pin-up girls of that time for the ploughboys. Later on the Misses Barlow started to sell them. Soon afterwards the comic postcards came in, and Barlow's bought a consignment, several of which were exhibited in the window. They caused quite a sensation, for some were saucy and others were sexy. In fact, a rumour went round the village that one of these was indecent. Everybody realised that the Misses Barlow would not know this, being very prim and proper.

The young people thought the subject funny, but the more Puritan section decided something must be done about it, and it was brought to the notice of Mrs Brown of the Manor. She realised that the Misses Barlow were unwittingly harbouring this offensive picture and, to save them any embarrassment, she went to the shop and said she wanted to buy a postcard to send to a relative. They brought out those they had in the shop, but she said she would like to see those in the window. There were four of these, and when they were handed to her, she could not decide which was the questionable one. So she bought the four, and the Missess Barlow never knew how near they had come to being involved in a moral scandal.

While the manor house was the class place of the village, the farm itself was generally considered to be poor. One prospective tenant said: 'The house is a good one.' The foreman replied: 'The house won't get you a living. The living should come off the land.'

It was split up into sections, one of which was around the village, and the other in the fens. Consequently it was difficult to make it pay, as it took the men the equivalent of two days a week to get to and from their work. Moreover, Mr Brown, in keeping with his position, did not try to get the last ounce as most others had to do, out of his employees. Unfortunately, he died during the depression in farming, and it was almost with a sense of humiliation that the villagers learned that his will had been proved at only a few thousand pounds. One of the men who was supposed to be near the family consoled us by saying that the will referred to his business only, and had nothing to do with his private fortune. Unfortunately, this proved to be incorrect.

The importance of the railway and our local railway station in my young days can hardly be appreciated by the children of the bus age.

This line was opened about ten years before I was born. Up to that time there seems to have been a sufficiency of labour for farmers, and there was a certain amount of casual labour available for the seasonal jobs.

When the railway was built, local labour was used on each particular section, and they paid 3d per day more than the average local wage. This attracted labourers from more permanent jobs

ncluding my father for a short period. When the line was completed, the permanent gang required from each village was
six platelayers; local signalmen and porters might be appointed if
hey had sufficient education. Father was offered a permanency
s a platelayer, which would have meant 1s a week extra and a
ıalf-day on Saturday, but he thought it a soulless job and his
ıeart was in the land. So he made what appeared to be a big
acrifice in turning down an easy, well-paid permanent job.

The railway station was the centre of all the commercial life
n the village. To us it was not a mere wayside station; it rep-
esented all the activity in the district. While there were stations
hree miles north and south on either side of it, east and west the
and disappeared into regions unknown. On the top side Gran-
ham had the nearest railway, twenty-five miles away, and on the
ow side there was only a branch line, about the same distance,
etween us and the sea. The main business came from within a
adius of about two miles, but there were also villages who had a
hoice of railways with whom we did much business. Billinghay,
large fen village, invariably used Digby, although they could
o to Scopwick.

At that time the station yard was a hive of industry from morn-
ng until night, with farmers bringing their produce and taking
way salt and chalk for the land, artificial manures, and indeed
ake for the cattle. There were also two firms which had depots
or coal, but the real glamour for us boys was at the passenger
tation. This was particularly busy on Mondays and Fridays, the
narket days of Sleaford and Lincoln respectively.

It was customary for the village people to be at the station
alf-an-hour before the train went, although most people could
valk it in five minutes. They went early for various reasons,
ne being that, slow in thought, it helped to compose their minds
or the journey. It also enabled them to get to know who else
vas going on the train, and if possible to find out why they were
oing. For instance, it was well known that one old lady went to
leaford for a special reason. She had a large family with whom
he very often quarrelled, and when she announced she was going
o Sleaford everybody knew why. She went only for one purpose

– to see her solicitor and change her will. One could usually te
by the relations seeing her off who was going to be left out. As sh
was supposed to be worth £1,000 it was news of importance t
the people concerned and to the village gossips.

Ten minutes before the train came in a big handbell was run
by the porter, and it was not considered good form to leave th
booking of a ticket until after that time, as the only bookin
clerk doubled his part as ticket collector also.

The station-master, Mr Fares, was a most important persor
When he condescended to drink at the Red Lion, he always aske
for a 'sensible', a local term for a quart. He was a big man an
always wore a frock coat with gold buttons and gold-braide
peaked cap. He looked dignified as he came out of his office to pa
his respects to the gentry in the first-class waiting-room, and afte
wards to escort them to their carriages. For the likes of us a no
from the station-master on these occasions was a special favou
What we called the gentry were two county families who lived i
nearby Halls. They came to the station in their carriage-and-pair
with coachmen and footmen. The farmers came in gigs an
dog carts, their children usually following in governess car
Most of the village knew who had gone by train. They also kne
by the ringing of the bell when the train was late.

When I was a boy, the thrill of a winter's evening was to g
down to the station to meet the 6.18 from Lincoln, when we use
to flash our bull's-eye lanterns on the dark road. The station itse
on a winter's night also provided warmth and light equal to th
public house, and of course it was free.

And then, for a small boy, there was always the policemar
I often heard our policeman's footsteps in the night. It was
friendly sound. This was an easy-going officer of an amiab
nature. He came from agricultural stock, he was built on th
heavy side, rather slow-witted, but his lot was not only a happ
but a very comfortable one. His beat extended to several sma
villages outside Digby, but with us he was very much one of th
family. We had a local saying, 'Yer know me, mate', which cam
in useful with him. In private life he was a good mixer, and was a
home either in chapel or the public house. He was also a goo

ardener and usually took one of the prizes for the best vegetable lisplay at the Feast.

We had no serious crime in the village, and certainly none of he inhabitants was ever arrested. The main transgression of the aw came from such incidents as riding without lights or riding vithout reins. It was quite common for a wagoner to sit on the hafts and direct his horses by word of mouth, especially if with lrink taken. There were also forgetful people who omitted to enew their dog or gun licences. Likewise, they were not permitted to shoot game with an ordinary gun licence, but this was omething to which the constable invariably turned a blind eye. A more serious matter that affected our family was a new regulaion of the period ordering a tablet to be fixed to all milk cans bearing the name and address of the owner, and the measures had to be certified correct. I delivered milk to the polceman's house and, like us, he could not see the sense of it. He decided to gnore the ordinance.

Any minor infringement was settled out of court over a glass of beer or whisky, if the severity of the case demanded it. A typical nstance was when the policeman had to see a gamekeeper about a dog that was supposed to be vicious. The gamekeeper lived in a onely spot, and he always enjoyed a bit of company. He fetched out the whisky bottle, and after a few drinks the policeman said he would like to see the animal. A word from the gamekeeper and the dog came out from under the couch; he put his muzzle n the policeman's hands and looked into his face. The constable patted the dog's head and said: 'You look a kind sort of a dog. really cannot summons you.' There the matter ended.

Of course it was necessary for him to put up a show and he lepended for his quota of court cases on what were to us foreigners' – people who came into the village on business. His nain source of arrests and summonses came from beggars who had no visible means of subsistence, and from gypsies who were either trespassing, stealing or hawking without a licence. I was called on upon many occasions to drive one of these prisoners to Sleaford, and I therefore considered myself to be almost attached o the Force. The only time I remember myself being found under suspicious circumstances was when I was with my elder brother gathering a large basket of mushrooms. As we came out of the field the policeman was leaning over the gate on which was the notice: 'Trespassers will be prosecuted'. As we approached my brother said: 'Now, mate, are you stopping 'em a bit like?' He replied: 'Aye, mate. Have you seen anybody about?' Nothing was said about our basket, but the policeman also had mushrooms for breakfast that morning.

It was always a schoolboy's ambition to own a bull's-eye lamp like the policeman's, but his had one advantage – he could make it flash red. It was an oil lamp attached to his belt, and on dark nights he used to like to shock people by flashing it in front of them as they came down the street.

It is not easy for a country policeman to work single-handed. There was an occasion on which he got two tramps and, as he could not manage them both, one of them got away. He handcuffed the one remaining to the roadman and went in pursuit of the other. When he eventually got the latter and brought him back, he found that the first one had slipped the handcuffs. The roadman said he had told the man he must not run away until the policeman came back, but he just swore at him and made off.

Of course, our local constable had several unpleasant jobs to do. He was always the man notified in cases of accidents, and where there was an inquest his house was often used as a temporary mortuary. It was also his job to escort any person going insane to the asylum. There was only one in my time.

It was a frightening affair that I shall never forget. I had heard that a woman had gone off her head in the next village, and that they would have to bring her past our house at a certain time next morning. Mother was out on her posting round, and I was told to remain in the house. However I heard a noise in the distance and I could not resist going to the gate. It was an ugly sight. The only means of conveyance in those days was by dogcart, and the woman was perched up between the policeman and an attendant, fighting and screaming. Her eyes were wild and her hair bedraggled. When she saw me she almost leapt out of the cart. I dashed back into the house, trembling, and locked the door.

The author's mother, in her ninety-eighth year

A family group on the hundredth birthday of the author's mother

The author on his ninetieth birthday, with his son and daughter

Although the policeman was settled in the village, he was pparently not much esteemed by his superiors, and he made an rror of judgment that seems to have reflected on the dignity and restige of the Force. Some labourers were going to their work t 6.30 in the morning and were hailed by the policeman from the op of a stack. They obtained a ladder to get him down, and the xplanation of his predicament caused much amusement in the ublic-house later. It appeared that, at dusk the previous night, he ad seen a ladder raised against the stack. On going to the top and nding a tramp, he brought him down and was taking him away hen the tramp said: 'Why have you left my mate up there?' The oliceman went back up the ladder, and when he turned round the dder was gone and the tramp was off.

After this, the powers-that-be, with the idea of restoring iscipline to the village, transferred him and sent down one of ieir bright young men who was out for promotion and, so far s he was concerned, Digby was only a stepping-stone to that end. Iy family were quickly involved. When I was delivering milk to is house, he wanted to know why the name was not on the can, nd why the measures had not been stamped. We were given a eek to have this done, but my parents decided it was neither ecessary nor economical to go to this expense, and decided to iscontinue delivering milk.

It did not make us any more popular in the policeman's eye hen he had to fetch his own. As a matter of interest, some fty years later, the farm which was supplying the milk has again opped deliveries because of a recent regulation that all delivered ilk must be bottled.

Fortunately in less than two years the policeman got his esired promotion and the whole village relaxed again. Perhaps ievitably, he became eventually a superintendent.

This officer was a petty tyrant, of no great ability in himself, but have always thought that the change to him from his easy-going redecessor was a sign of a very big change in the relationship etween the public and centralised authority.

To return to the gentry of the great days of landowning . . . one ic Bailey has provided me with some fine stories out of his vast treasury of local knowledge. I reprint these much as h wrote them out for me in old-fashioned exercise books.

The local gentry were all Justices of the Peace. The Bloxholr squire used to be driven by his coachman into Sleaford each wee to sit on the bench at the Session House or Police Court. On evening, when he wanted to go home, the coachman had got to drunk to drive, so the Squire left him in Sleaford and got on th box of the brougham and drove home himself. When the carriag pulled up at the Hall front the butler came out, opened th carriage door, and saw no one inside. It was dark, so he looked u to the box and said: 'Where have you left the old b—?' He wa flabbergasted when the Squire's voice said: 'Tell the grooms t come and fetch the brougham.' When they had done so th Squire walked through the front door, the butler after him.

The butler said: 'Sir, after what I have said, all I can do is to giv you a month's notice.' 'Nonsense!' said the Squire. 'We all mak mistakes.' The butler said: 'I have broke my own heart, an although you are one of the best employers, I shall never be abl to look you straight in the face any more.' He left the job and th boss got him a better post than ever.

The footman married the ladies' maid. My father had give them some wood pigeons. The newly married couple asked fathe and mother to supper. They asked father to carve the roaste pigeons. He started, and said: 'Why, the insides are still in!' Th footman raved. His wife said: 'Don't blame me. I told you I ha never cooked in my life, but you were determined to marry me Things were smoothed out, and they had a good evening.

One racehorse won the St Leger at Doncaster, 1875, the Oaks a Epsom, the 1,000 Guineas at Newmarket and the Coronation Stake at Ascot. Apology belonged to Mr Kinge of Ashby Hall, wh owned Ashby-de-la-Launde estate and also was Vicar of Ashby fo fifty-three years. His uncle was Vicar before him for thirty year One Mr Kinge was shut up in the Tower of London and fine £50,000 by Cromwell. The Bishop of Lincoln remonstrated wit Mr Kinge for keeping racehorses, though they were registered i his wife's name. Mr Kinge sent a card to the Bishop and wrote on only one word, 'Apology'. She won the four races in one season.

II

PRIVATE ENTERPRISE

New times demand new measures and new men
The world advances and in time outgrows
The laws that in our fathers' day were best:
And, doubtless, after us, some purer scheme
Will be shaped out by wiser men than we,
Made wiser by the steady growth of truth.

J. R. LOWELL

'he three trades that were most affected through new enterprise
ı the 'nineties were the grocer's and general dealer, the boot-
ıaker and the tailor. The first encroachment by competitors
ame from the bakers.

When our chief shopkeeper, Mr Barlow, died the village had up
ɔ that time been almost self-contained. Barlow's shop provided
early all the necessities of life in the way of food, apart from what
ıe villagers grew themselves. He left three grown-up daughters,
ho continued the business, with the exception of baking bread
nd supplying offal for pig feed. Eventually, one of the daughters
ıarried; the two remaining sisters, Miss Jennie and Miss Lizzie,
arried on.

The shop stood in a favoured position in the centre of the
illage. Inside there were three counters. At the one next to the
indow, sweets and tobacco were served. Opposite the door was
ıe general grocery, and at the rear the general drapery. Their
ving-room was down a passage, and as the shop door opened a
ell rang and they seemed to appear out of a tunnel. Although it
ould only be a few yards long it must have meant several hours
alking every week. We used to watch to see which of them
ould emerge from the darkness. Miss Jennie was the favourite;
ıe always had a pleasant smile, and if we were buying a half-

pennyworth of sweets she invariably threw in an extra one fc make-weight.

Lizzie was plainer and more matter-of-fact. She always appeare to have a weight on her mind, and served us indifferently a a mere duty. I knew almost every article in the shop throug waiting for Miss Biddy Brown's order on Saturday mornings One picture has remained in my mind. It was of a jovial ma sitting at a table in the process of carving a large succulent piec of beef. A caption underneath said: 'Colman's Mustard'.

The shop was always spick and span, and the sisters appeare to serve alternately during the day-time, but in the evening the were both in the shop and put on special dresses. They also bot served on Saturdays. I don't know at what hours the shop wa open, but I never passed it as a boy when it was closed, althoug the shop was just around the corner from us. The light reflecte on the road at night, and before I got to it it gave me a sort c feeling of safety; and when I left the light coming away, I alway made a dash for home. Their window was the only light showin anywhere in the village. I imagine they kept open until nin o'clock every night, and probably much later on Saturdays, bu most people including ourselves were in bed long before that.

Most of the shop window was filled with sweets, but the displa of the year took place just before Christmas when it would b gaily decorated with small presents, toys, crackers and sugar pigs These last were the favourites with children, especially when the were brought out in various colours. I personally never remembe having a toy which, except for spinning tops, seemed a waste c money. We put out stockings at Christmas, but they were fille only with apples, oranges, nuts and sugar pigs.

As the Misses Barlow no longer baked bread, this was th opportunity for a baker in the nearby village of Ruskington t come to Digby with a bread cart. He also brought pig meal an groceries, and gradually obtained a substantial amount of trade i the village, introducing small luxuries such as oranges an tomatoes. I remember once buying three oranges for 1d, but w never aspired to tomatoes, which were said to be an acquire taste.

No sooner had this competitor become established than a bigger one came into the field. This was the Co-operative Stores, which were paying 1s 4d and 1s 8d in the £1 dividend on all purchases except offal. The private traders had fought hard to keep the stores out, but eventually they obtained a footing in the village. My parents were among the first to join, and ever afterwards they were very enthusiastic Co-op members and made the dividends part of their savings.

It seems interesting that all the representatives of the firms that did business with the village in those days were local preachers. Peetman, the baker from Ruskington, would no doubt know the Barlows very well, and he came to Digby in the first place with the idea of collaborating. The manager of the Stores at Metheringham, a large village in the opposite direction, was also well known as a local preacher. The first insurance man who did business was likewise a local preacher. Later, other forces came into play, and this subtle method of gaining confidence became out of date.

It was sad to notice the quick decline in the trade of the Misses Barlows' shop. As competition came into the village and their stock got old, some of it almost went mouldy on the shelves. They did not even understand the new methods, and could not replace it. They were continually asked for things they had not got, and later they could not afford to buy the sort of things they were accustomed to getting. Trade dwindled until people said: 'It's no use going to Barlows, they won't have it.' I only remember them making two errors of judgment – one I have already mentioned in connection with the postcards, and one that was more serious as a reflection on their business sagacity.

The biggest dunce in the school was a big boy from Bloxholm. Unfortunately, he had to stay longer than us because he could not pass any exams. I used to help him with his sums and spelling in exchange for walnuts, apples and pears, which he collected from the Hall park on his way to school.

One morning this boy came to school with the exciting news that on the way he had picked up a half-sovereign. He decided to spend it and went to Miss Barlow's. He told his story, which they might not have accepted if he had tried to spend all the money straight away, but seeing that he only wanted to spend 3d, they imagined he would take the other 9s 9d home. The lad had other ideas. This was the time to repay all his friends for all their various kindnesses, so he asked them all what they would like to have and gave them the money to get it. In my case it was a knife which cost 1s.

Late that night there was a knock on the door; the boy's father came to enquire what was my share of the spoils. Unfortunately I had not told my parents what had happened, and I had to produce the knife which, along with every other tangible asset, was taken back to the shop and the money had to be returned. It appeared that the boy had taken the half-sovereign from his father's pocket. It took some time for the Misses Barlow to live down this lapse, and ever afterwards any child who brought a half-sovereign to the shop would have to produce a letter from the parents.

In their own small world in the room at the back of the shop they lived a very secluded life. Although I delivered milk there every morning for several years I never once saw their living-room, which was separated from the back door by the kitchen; and although the window of the living-room fronted directly onto North Street, it was difficult to see in through the screen of net. Sometimes in the winter twilight, the fire gave glimpses of a cheerful, cosy room with comfortable furniture, a well-filled book case and silver on the tea table.

The next two trades to feel the effects of outside competition were the bootmaker and the tailor. This competition came from multiple stores then being established in Lincoln.

Vess Upton was the village bootmaker and cobbler. In my early years he was at the peak of his prosperity. In appearance he was a John Bull type of man, comfortable-looking, with side-whiskers, well-fed and reputed to have a good bank balance, although at his death some years later it had dwindled to very little.

Vess made the boots for most of the men who worked on the land in our district, and it was the usual thing for a boy leaving school to start off with a pair of 'Vess and Jim's'. One of the advantages of buying from Upton was that it could be paid for out of the first year's earnings, received on May Day. The first thing a ploughboy did was to go to pay the bill at the tailor's and the bootmaker's.

The boots were supposed to last three years without letting water in. They were ugly, heavy, hobnailed, and rather crudely made, but they did serve their purpose, which was most important to men having to work ankle-deep in mud in winter.

Vess had other interests apart from trade. He was a good shot and very friendly with the local gamekeepers. He also held an important position as gun-loader for gentry who came to shoot in the district. This enabled him to mix in two worlds. He made his living out of the poor people, but there was always an air of condescension in his dealings with them. For the best part of the year they might be in his debt, and his customers were treated as though he was doing them a favour. He was also a sidesman at the church, and one of the leading lights in the Red Lion bar. When given the job of making the presentation to the vicar's warden for forty years' continuous service he made what was perhaps the shortest speech ever made in the village. In handing over the gift he simply said: 'That's it!'

The bootmaker's shop was a hotbed of gossip. No rumour was too far-fetched to receive credence there. He kept no stock of boots. They had to be ordered well in advance, and taking and fetching boots gave most people the opportunity of listening to or retailing the gossip of the day. The smallest bit of it would be chewed over until the last drop of juice was extracted from it.

As you entered the shop Vess himself sat on one stool, Jimmy North slightly behind him. Jimmy was very much a 'yes-man', and after Vess had told the most impossible yarn he always turned to Jimmy and said, 'Isn't that so Jimmy?' who always replied: 'Aye, mester.' I myself have heard these two expressions scores of times. Vess had a way of putting words into people's mouths. Once when I was in, a man came to report that his boots nipped a bit. Vess said: 'You must be a strange liar, Graves. When I saw you last week you only said how comfortable they were.' Graves said afterwards that he thought of retorting sharply to that, but didn't like.

But Vess's throne was already toppling. Vague rumours began

to float around that a shop had opened in Lincoln called the Public Benefit Shoe Shop and that labourers' boots could be bought at 13s 6d a pair, less than half the price of Vess Upton's, which cost 30s. At first this was ridiculed, while Vess claimed that they were 'nothing but brown paper' and wouldn't last a week of clod-hopping. Eventually someone did actually buy a pair, and to everybody's astonishment they were waterproof and wore well. Moreover, they were less heavy, better-made and much more comfortable.

Up until then only boots had been worn by men and women, but at this time shoes were introduced and became popular for Sunday wear. My mother, who had already fallen for one of the new-fangled notions by joining the Co-op, was immediately on the war path and decided that father should try a pair. He did so, and from then on there was a change in the atmosphere when I came into contact with Vess Upton. The crisis came when I took him a pair of father's boots to be soled and heeled and he refused, saying that machine-made boots were not worth repairing.

The tailor, Sumner Brown, employed two other men, and also kept a large stock of cloth at the back of a very pleasant shop.

Everybody was very sorry for Sum Brown when his trade declined as, being a cripple with no legs, he had nothing else to turn to. Moreover, he was a very pleasant man and a good workman, but he just could not compete in his slow methods with machine-made suits at 25s each. There was a new style with the multiple suits and, although they were not strongly made, they had a better finish. They also offered other shades than the indigo blue which was Sumner's only line for Sunday wear. The only week-day clothes were ready-made corduroys.

12

GROCER'S ASSISTANT

The hours we pass with happy prospects in view are more pleasing than those crowned with fruition, in the first we cook the dishes to our appetite in the latter nature cooks it for us.

GOLDSMITH

lthough the schoolmaster was conscientious and hard-working, cannot remember anything in particular I learned from him. he size of the class made it necessary for him to concentrate ainly on reading, writing and arithmetic.

I failed to pass the Labour examination, which would have abled me to leave school at twelve. This was a surprise to verybody, for I was considered one of the brightest boys in the hool. It happened because I was placed next to the examiner, ho kept up a most interesting discussion with the schoolmaster n the philosophy of Herbert Spencer. I did not understand a word ey said but was fascinated by listening to their voices. It was e first time I had heard cultured people talk, and it brought to fe something I had only read about in novelettes.

I never read any of the prize books I got at the Sunday-school. hese usually had such titles as *Captain of the School,* but on one ccasion I was given a book which a woman with literary tastes in e village told me I ought never to have been given, as it was a assic.

This remark which I did not understand, persuaded me to look rough it. The book was *Eugene Aram* by Lord Lytton. I did not nderstand it, but I always afterwards remembered one sentimental ntence which appealed to my romantic mind. It occurred when e hero was sitting on a tree stump, looking unkempt and elancholy, and the beautiful daughter of the squire came along nd said: 'You're not in distress, I hope?' He replied: 'No, Madam.

If by distress you mean beggary, I am perhaps, in all respect
better than I appear.'

I left school some time before I was thirteen, and entered th
grocery trade as an apprentice. My mother had the simple bu
definite ambition implied in my title that none of her sons shoul
have dirty boots, the bugbear, from a woman's point of view, c
working on the land. In any case it was at best a mere existenc
Besides, I had a peculiar reason of my own for not wanting t
work on the land. It seems so trivial that I do not think I hav
mentioned it before to anyone. I have a curious but instinctiv
dislike of handling dry soil. So long as my hands are in dam
soil I am all right, but as soon as the soil dries on my hands m
blood runs cold. Even today I cannot bear to watch the gardene
rub his hands if he has touched dry earth.

In choosing grocery for me my parents were influenced by th
fact that I should be where food was sold, and that there would b
plenty of it. The arrangement was that I should live in and ge
1s 3d per week spending money.

My parents had had unfortunate experiences with two of m
older brothers. The eldest was apprenticed to a blacksmith in th
village, a poor man with a large family. In consequence there wa
so little to eat that, in the words of the Bible, 'he would fain hav
filled his belly with the husks that the swine did eat'. My brothe
has told me that he often ate turnips out of the fields. He ra
away on two occasions because he was hungry. Running awa
was a common gesture of apprentices and other tied farr
workers. In those days it was equivalent to going on strike.

The next brother, who was apprentice to the village carpente
lived at home and got 3s a week for the first year, rising to 5s th
next. This was an even bigger strain on the family budget fo
however cheap and coarse the food, it was impossible to keep
healthy growing young man on the sum. Moreover, both m
brothers had to have special tools and clothing for their trades.

So the brother next to me was apprenticed to a baker, on th
principle that where there was bread there must be sufficient food
the same reasoning that applied when I went into the grocer
trade. In practice this theory did not work out according t

:pectations. Neither of us turned out as strong and healthy as the ʋo brothers who had less to eat.

Choice of trades in the village was limited. Apart from the acksmith and carpenter, we had a saddler, tailor, bootmaker ıd butcher. The last was in those days not merely a purveyor of eat; he had to be strong enough to kill an ox every week. None ˙ our family aspired to butchery. The tailoring and bootmaking ısinesses were declining because – as I have said in the previous ıapter – ready-mades were coming into fashion and because three :w multiple shops had opened in Lincoln. These were a boot ıop, a 25s tailor and a cycle shop. They caused quite a sensation the time, and I went on a half-day excursion just to look in their indows.

When my younger brother was ready to start work the choice ˙ trades was exhausted. Having tasted the sweets of government rvice my mother became Civil Service-minded and was very ıxious that my two younger brothers should become members ˙ that select body. The brother next to me in age inherited the ɔok round. It had continued to prosper, and when I left home ıe goodwill was assessed at £2 10s. This brother made a great ıccess of it; he did not waste time reading the books but used the ːofits to pay for a high-school education in Lincoln. There is no ɔubt that the money earned from the book round contributed aterially to both my younger brothers' education. My brother tended the Lincoln school until he was fifteen. At the same time, ıis caused a strain on the family economy. Apart from school fees ıere was the cost of the season ticket on the railway, lunch, ɪecial clothing and other incidentals. Also, in the normal way, boy would be going to work and earning money at that age.

It was a great day when, at the age of fifteen, my brother went London to sit for a Boy Clerks' examination. Mother no doubt ıought this was the end of that liability; it was unthinkable that : should not pass. Whereas, although he had apparently qualified ɪr an appointment, several hundred others had done the same, ıd there were only 150 vacancies. The appointments were made om those with the highest marks, and if more were required ıey were appointed in order of marks until the next examination

was held. As my brother did not hear anything he had to s
again, with the same result.

Up till then the family had been in the dark as to how the
vacancies were filled. Mother, however, found that by paying 4
a list of the markings could be obtained. This showed that m
brother was only a few marks off success. It also disclosed that h
had received only 60 marks out of a possible 200 for Englis
Composition. This got mother's back up and she immediately s
down and wrote a strong letter to the Civil Service Commissione
in which she told them the examiners must have made a mistak
she had evidence that this was my brother's best subject, an
suggested that the marks should have read 160 and not 60. If s
he should already have been offered a post. More than that, sh
pointed out that the boy was heart and soul for the Civil Servic
and that they had scraped and scraped all their lives to provide th
necessary education for him, and would they please look into th
matter at once and rectify the mistake?

Imagine the triumph of the family when, shortly afterward
my brother was posted to the War Office. Alas, he discovere
soon after reaching London that the position had been filled
the natural order of selection! Needless to say, nothing was said
home to detract from mother's achievement.

There was no doubt that he had won the brighter boots in th
family, and he was to add much polish to them later.

My brother's commencing salary was 15s a week, out of whic
he always saved 1s, after having paid 12s for his lodgings wi
a policeman. On the day of his appointment mother received
rise of 3d a week from the Post Office, and this she said she wou
put aside to save up for her first trip to London.

As for my brother's career in London, he has often amused m
by relating how, when he arrived in the capital as a raw boy fro
the country, a colleague tactfully informed him that a cloth ca
was hardly the proper wear for a budding Civil Servant. H
promptly went out and bought himself a bowler for half a crow

When he left the village the book round passed on to th
youngest brother of all, and he paid for his schooling mainly ou
of the commission until he was nearly twenty years of age. He als

began his career in the Civil Service, but left it later and is now a successful farmer. When he in turn gave up the round, my mother took it over and many years later it passed to my niece. It is now out of the family, but still prospering.

As for myself between the ages of thirteen and twenty, I have nothing good to report. I would like to rule out this period by describing it as seven 'years that the locusts have eaten', but perhaps I should give an impression of it to show the state of my mind at the age of twenty, when I emerged from the chrysalis stage.

I had heard a lot about the young man for whom I was going to work and the prospect appealed to my adventurous nature. He was the son of a wholesale grocer in Lincoln, and he had been to a public school. Unfortunately, on leaving school and going into his father's business, he got into wild company and started to drink. He had therefore been put under the care of my brother's boss, a grocer and baker, a strict disciplinarian, for a year's probation. The young man wanted to get married, and it was understood that if he worked and could keep off drink for a year his father would buy a business for him. When I began working for him this probationary period was over; he had married and bought the grocery side of the baker's business, together with the goodwill of various country rounds that had been worked up.

For a short time everything went well. He had married a good-looking and charming girl and they seemed to be very happy. He was fond of horse riding, but he did little work in the shop, which was managed by a capable assistant. Under this assistant there was a boy about sixteen, an improver, and myself. We all three lived in. We did notice that our employer was rather weak, and that people took advantage of him. He was often swapping horses, but he was no judge of their good points and usually got the worst of the bargain.

On one occasion he bought a horse from the saddler in the next village and found on arrival home that it had got the staggers. I was given the unpleasant job of riding the horse back about four miles to leave it with a note for the saddler. Knowing what an unfriendly man the saddler was, I dreaded what he would say or do, and I was relieved to find his shop closed for dinner, although he lived only next door. I got off the horse and quickly tied it to the ring on the shop, went to the door of the house, slipped the note through the letter box and started for home. I hadn't gone more than 100yd before I heard the saddler shouting after me, but I pretended not to hear.

After I had gone about a mile I was caught up by the saddler's apprentice on the horse. He told me that I had to take it back to my boss. I said I had instructions not to do so, and he said: 'Well I've got to hand it back so you might as well ride behind me.' I did so and got off just before we reached our village. My boss gave me instructions to take it back again, so of course I gave the saddler's boy a lift. We continued doing this all day. I cannot now remember who eventually kept the horse.

We took a van round the countryside. This was a shop on wheels. It was built round a 100gal paraffin tank, similar to the modern petrol tanks but on a smaller scale. When we started the day and the tank was full it was much too heavy for one horse, so a single shaft was put in the middle and we had two horses. This was not very successful. As they pulled, they were drawn together so much that they leaned on each other with their feet outwards, and if the road was at all slippery they fell to the ground, and of course always broke the shaft. This meant we were held up a lot for repairs. In consequence we were late, people could not rely on us, and we lost a lot of custom.

After a few months the chief assistant left and was not replaced, which meant that the sixteen-year-old boy and I had to manage the best way we could. Up to this time there had at least been somebody in the shop who could tidy up and prepare things for the van the following day. Now, of course, everything was in confusion. We had to work at night or in the early morning to get the van loaded, and the shop was in a state of chaos, with sides of bacon, groceries, oil and corn all mixed up.

One night when we came home we heard the disconcerting news that the boss's father was expected the following day. It was the first time he had been to the shop, and the boss decided that we must clear it up and make it respectable. To encourage us he ffered to work all night. It was certainly a sight in the village for he shop to be lit up. We got the help of two strong men to assist n moving the sacks of corn and sides of bacon into the roadway o make a clean start. One of these chaps was a big hefty fellow nd in by-play the boss challenged him to carry a 16-stone sack n his back home (nearly half a mile away) without stopping. f he could do this he could keep it. This, of course, the man did uite easily. While this was going on, the other man, not to be utdone, took home a side of bacon. Anyway, we worked hroughout the night, filled the shelves and made the shop look resentable. Next day the inspection passed off satisfactorily.

After this things went from bad to worse, and eventually the ther boy left. Now that I was the only employee with the xception of the horseman, my employer had to come with me on he round. It needed two people, not only to manage the horses, ut also for the sake of mere cleanliness. One of us was supposed o attend to the groceries and the other to serve the paraffin and oils.

It happened, unfortunately, that the boss had started drinking gain and went straight to the public-house in any village, while attended to the customers. As I was handling the oil, the butter nd cheese soon acquired a new flavour. We used to collect the armers' home-made butter and credit the value against groceries.

This was quite important to the success or failure of a country usiness. The village people knew who made the best butter and ought it. The good grocer was discriminating about which butter e took, and while we had a large trade most of our butter came rom farms that other grocers would not deal with, and we made o difference in the market price. Farmers' butter in any case was lways strong at buttercup time. On many occasions we would xchange groceries worth £1 for butter that could not be sold. We used it later for greasing the cartwheels.

My employer provided a certain amount of entertainment in the village inns. He had strong teeth, between which he could bend nd twist any ordinary piece of metal. One of his specialities was o take a gold coin from a fob which he carried on his watch chain nd bend it into various shapes. Then, if he was in the mood, he would throw it on the floor and leave it there. Several times

I have seen people asking him to straighten out coins that he had thrown away on a previous occasion. By this time, he was spending most of the takings, and things were reaching a climax.

The worst journey I had with him was on a Saturday. We arrived with the van at a large village about six miles from home. There was a football match in the afternoon, and the local team were a man short. They asked my boss if he would play for them. He decided to cancel the rest of the day's journey to do so. After the match they all adjourned to the local, and I had to wait for him until about midnight. When at last he came out, he had obviously had a lot to drink. He face was white and tense.

I shall never forget the drive. It was a nightmare, and we were very lucky to get back alive. He took the reins as if he were possessed and drove like a madman. He thrashed the horses at full gallop the whole way. Long before we reached home you could not see their coats for white lather. We were fortunate not to meet anyone on the way, as the van rocked and surged so much that we could have turned over. Before we reached the last turning into the village I appealed to him to slow down. He refused and we passed the turning at full gallop. I remember starting to fight him for the reins. All at once he handed them over and said very calmly: 'Well, Fred, do as you like.' I gradually pulled the horses up and got down trembling. I refused to get back into the van and walked the horses all the way to the village.

The night was not yet over. Having reached home, I was having some food in the kitchen before going to bed when the bell rang. The boss and his wife were in the sitting-room, finishing a meal. On the table was a small heap of gold coins – sovereigns and half-sovereigns. He told me to sit down and said: 'Well, who do you think was the best footballer on the field, Fred, to-day?' The general opinion had been that he was the best, so I said so. He replied: 'Well, here's a pound for you, but don't tell Harry.' (Harry was the horseman.) He went on talking for a little while and then asked me again who was the best footballer on the field. I said the same thing, and he handed me another pound. This went on for at least a quarter of an hour, during which the mistress never said a word. In the end he handed all the money over. I ent to bed with £8. I had to hand the lot back the next morning.

We were now living in a state of crisis. At home, while I had ot referred to the state of the business, I had mentioned, in all nocence, that I was carrying 16-stone sacks of corn. My parents isisted on my leaving. They were not much concerned about hat I had to eat or my working conditions; it was thought in the ountry that no boy should carry a 16-stone sack until he was ixteen years of age, or the consequences would be permanently ıjurious.

The end came quickly after I left the grocer. There was nobody o do the round, and I do not remember whether my employer ent bankrupt or made a composition, but I know they were educed to very poor circumstances.

Fifteen years later I heard that they were living in a nearby illage, and I went to visit them. The wife still had traces of charm nd good looks, but she had aged considerably. They lived in a ery poor farm cottage, and he was in a small outhouse, in the st stages of tuberculosis. The wife told me that their child was lready working as a farmer's boy in the fields.

I had been in the grocery business about fifteen months, having earned nothing about the trade except the names and prices of a w goods. The motto on the van was 'Small Profits, Quick eturns', and I remember that we bought large consignments of ertain things to sell as specialities. For instance, on one occasion ne boss bought a ton of currants and sold them at 1d per lb. He lso bought a truckload of matches, which were retailed at 1d a ozen or 8½d for twelve dozen. As many of the calls we made ere out of the way, and we only went once a week, I had to nemorise for the benefit of customers all the goods they might equire – tea, sugar, coffee, cocoa, soap, sodas, washing powders, lues, beeswax and turpentine.

Socially I mixed with the sort of people that I had been brought p with. There were no recreational facilities, and I went to hapel as I did at home. The leading light at the chapel was the ther village grocer and draper, our only competitor.

Theirs was an old-established firm. They had a very pleasant ouse adjoining the shop and several charming daughters, with one of whom our chief assistant fell in love. Owing to the busines rivalry, however, he was not encouraged, and I think that ma have been the reason he left the village. While driving the van h used to sing a mournful song about being jilted. The chorus use to haunt me.

> And now she's happy with another,
> One that has bright gold in store.
> It was her that caused my heart to ponder,
> I'm left alone because I'm poor.

I had one embarrassing moment at the chapel, when I wa asked to give a recitation at the Sunday-school Anniversary. chose a rather exciting poem about a railway engine driver goin mad at the controls, but I was unable to learn the whole of i before the day. So I had to get up and give as much as I knew then apologise just at the climax of the story, when the drive tells the fireman: 'I will drive to Eternity.' I must have had a ver odd mentality in those days.

I made my first social contact on the same Sunday afternoon The improver in our store had bought a pair of kid gloves whic were too small for him. He carried them about, however, and o this occasion, in order to improve my status, he kindly lent m one. We met two girls from the next village and, as far as know, it was the first time I had shaken hands. I remember that had nothing whatever to say.

Most people in their lives have a narrow escape from death It was during this period that I had my narrowest shave. On very hot Sunday an older boy asked me to go with him for bathe in a nearby river. I told him I could not swim, but he sai that was quite all right; he would teach me. He explained how t swim simply by jumping in and striking out for the side. I jumpe in and of course went straight to the bottom. After a grea struggle I managed to get to the bank, only to find that m instructor had got entangled in the weeds. I threw my coat to hin and managed to pull him out. Later the same day a boy in th village was drowned in almost the same spot.

13
UP THE LADDER

If you wish in this world to advance
Your merits you're bound to enhance;
  You must stir it and stump it
  And blow your own trumpet
Or, trust me, you haven't a chance.

SIR W. S. GILBERT (*Ruddigore*)

After leaving the grocer, I arrived back home to find that father had gone into the carting business.

We now had two horses and carts, and he had got a contract for leading the stones used to repair the roads. I came in very handy to look after one of the horses. This suited me, but mother said it was a dead end and insisted that I went back to learning a trade. So in due course it was arranged for me to go to a larger grocery and drapery store in a village about twenty miles away. I was to live in and receive 1s 6d per week for two years.

In the first place I was sent to a small branch shop where the staff consisted of only a manager, a girl on the drapery side, myself and an errand boy. This errand boy was quite a character. The story was that he had been sacked one Saturday night for being cheeky. Nevertheless he turned up next Monday morning and was taking down the shutters as usual when the manager came out and said: 'I thought I gave you the sack on Saturday night Jack?' The boy replied: 'Yes you did, and don't do it again. I got into the devil of a row when I got home.' He was re-engaged.

I was the only person living in. It was very inconvenient. There was only one living-room, the manager and his wife were newly married, and I felt somewhat in the way. It was winter time, I could not go out, and I went straight to bed every night. So far as

I remember, I did not speak to a soul outside the shop during the three months I was there. I think it could not have been doing very much trade because I remember nothing about the customers

When I was transferred to the main shop I certainly made up for my lack of social life, for this place was a hive of activity and gossip. There were three other apprentices and three assistants Over us all was the first assistant, who understood both grocery and drapery. He was reputed to get a wage of £1 a week. We al lived in, except the girls in the drapery, who lived in the village Apart from the seven shop employees, the family consisted of the boss, his wife, five children of school age and three maids. should think the total wage bill for the ten employees living in would be under £4 a week.

The family had their own rooms, but these I did not see during the two years I was there. We lived in the kitchen and slept in very large, rambling attics. We had three rooms among the seven of us. The bell rang every morning in our room at seven, and it was my job to waken the others. Their attic was over anothe part of the house, and I had to go through the store-room where I always remember there was a smell of rotten apple. In the winter, by the light of the candle, I could see rats scampering away

The food in the house was reasonably good, and we supple mented it with tins of milk from the warehouse. The young men in the shop were a decent set. We had not much time to go astray for we worked from eight in the morning to eight at night (nine at night on Fridays and eleven at night on Saturdays). But we did get a half-day on Wednesdays, when we often walked to the nearest town four miles away.

Every day we had a round to do in the country but Monday when I went with the first assistant, was the heaviest. We wer loaded up and off by 7.30am and never arrived back before nine or ten at night. Half way, we had a break for lunch, while the horses were changed and the van replenished.

One of our customers was a man who was either too fat to walk or had lost the use of his legs. He always crawled out to see us his watch chain and waistcoat trailing on the ground. He went about in a nursery trap, half lying down inside. Another custome was a very hefty woman farmer who employed a lot of Irishmen. When we arrived there, they used to stand round while she bought a side or two of bacon. Then she would cut off chunks, hand them to the Irishmen without weighing and charge them what she thought fit.

We had two peculiar experiences in this district, strangely enough in successive weeks. It was winter time and pitch dark. As we approached a farmhouse we heard the weirdest noises. A hundred voices seemed to be groaning and moaning at once, intermingled with the banging of what turned out to be pots and pans and all sorts of domestic and farming implements. As we got nearer we could see that the house was completely surrounded by people with flares.

They were indulging in the local custom of 'rantanning' the occupiers. They were a sort of vigilance society who showed up people who were misbehaving. In this case it was common knowledge that the farmer's wife entertained a neighbouring farmer every time her husband was away, and this was the occasion of one of his nocturnal visits. I don't know how long the rantanning was kept up, but it must have been very embarrassing for the couple inside.

On the following Monday night, when we approached the same farm, we could see in the distance flames shooting up from the stackyard. Within a very short time the whole of the year's harvest was destroyed. I don't think this had anything to do with the previous week's events, but it was a strange coincidence.

Mondays were always tiring days for me. After the last call had been made, usually four to five miles from home, I used to creep into the van and fall asleep until we got back. There was generally a very pleasant treat in store for us – a supper of fried bacon and fried potatoes. We usually took £100 on a Monday, and that was a lot of money in those days.

The most fascinating people who came to the shop were travellers. One in particular the apprentices always rushed to take to the boss. He carried no samples. He wore a top hat and frock coat and carried an umbrella. He never asked for business and made only a courtesy call, but he gave 2s 6d to the boy who took the message to the boss. He was the aristocrat of travellers. He represented Colman's Mustard.

At a rival shop the owner was in some financial difficulties. A certain traveller called and sent in his name. The owner sent back word that he could not see him. The traveller told the boy to go back and say that he had come to see the owner and intended to stay until he had done so. The message came back that the traveller was to go to Hell. To this the traveller replied: 'You go back and tell your boss I've come to Hell. I've come to see the old devil, and I will see him before I go away.' The boss replied 'It's all right Jack, I'll see him.'

The family at our shop were very high church, and it was the mistress's ambition to save the soul of every member of the staff. We were persuaded and cajoled into being confirmed, and although I pointed out that I was already a member of the chapel, she did not think this was sufficient for my salvation. I had to be confirmed along with the other juniors.

We always had to go to church on Sunday, and on one occasion during the singing of a hymn a young man standing next to me fell to the floor. He was carried out. Everyone thought he must have had a fit. When we came out of church it was a dark night and one of the wildest I can remember. As another assistant and myself were struggling down the street we met someone who told us that the young man in church had dropped down dead.

I turned round to say something to the boy I was with and saw him falling to the ground. It was a weird sensation. I felt myself going too and started to run. I ran into the church wall with my head, and that soon brought me to my senses. My companion had only fainted, but the other young man was dead.

I served the two years to complete my apprenticeship at this place, and then, when I was sixteen, I obtained a job as an improver with a multiple store. I was paid 17s 6d a week, which left me 5s 6d after paying 12s for lodgings. I also had to pay 6d a week to the newly-formed Shop Assistants' Union. There I needed to know all the things I had not learned in my previous job but, fortunately, they also wanted someone to work up business in the outlying villages, and in that department I was the only one who could lay claim to any experience.

This firm specialised in giving presents with tea. As samples I carried two cups and saucers and a tea kettle; the customer could choose which to take. They were given away with a quarter of a pound of tea, price 7d. Under the scheme it was also possible to save up the tea wrappers and so get much more expensive presents. In one particular case a woman had accumulated a large number of wrappers. Her daughter was getting married, and she came to choose, as presents, useful things for the bride. One was a chamberpot, and after taking several other articles she was hesitating about having a second one. Our manager began to lose patience and at last exploded: 'I'll tell you what it is Mrs Soanso. Buy another quarter-pound of tea, and you can have a closet.'

This manager was the only man I remember meeting before I was twenty who tried to educate himself. He used to make a study of words, and on Sunday in church he wrote on his celluloid cuffs all the words he did not understand. On Monday morning he would pull off his cuffs and look up the words in the dictionary. He retired in 1951 and became a prominent man in his locality.

I was eighteen months with the multiple store and then, at the age of eighteen, I left to work for a young man who was just starting his own grocery business.

My new employer was an ambitious person with plenty of vitality. He always started any conversation with: 'What I mean, I mean, I mean, I mean.' He was also a stickler for punctuality. The job that I got had been advertised a month earlier, and I remarked when he engaged me that he had been a long time in making up his mind. He said: 'Actually I did put another man on, but he only stayed a fortnight. The first week he was a minute late one morning, and before the next week was out he was three minutes late, I couldn't stand that.'

The sequel was amusing, for I had such success in working up the rounds that when, at the end of three months, my landlady came down to enquire where I was and to leave some message, he replied that he didn't know where I was. If I was on the Saxby round I should be lying under the trees with two girls, and if I was on the Mabelthorpe round I should be playing skittles on the sands. This seems to indicate that I had converted him from his obsession with punctuality.

I was in this job about a year. Then I was tempted by the assistant superintendent of an insurance company to take over a book. It was supposed to bring in a guinea a week commission. I accepted this. Up till then I had been more or less under the discipline of working certain hours of the day. Now, for the first time, I was free for at least two or three days in the week.

I started well and got a fair amount of new business, but I seemed to work out the area quickly. It was not like having something fresh to offer every week, and I found that I had a lot of time on my hands. Through associating with other insurance agents who were in the same position, I started to play cards, first nap and then solo. Soon this absorbed all my spare time, and on one occasion, when the assistant superintendent's wife was away, five of us played for two days and a night.

I soon realised this job was doing me no good, and that I must get away from the gambling environment. I therefore took another insurance job at Lincoln, and in so doing jumped out of the frying pan into the fire. It was the worst experience of my life.

First of all I made the silly mistake of getting lodgings for 11s a week instead of the usual 12s. The extra 1s would have made all the difference. To start with, there were four of us sleeping in one bedroom. The front of the house was occupied by two girl assistants who were visited by gentlemen friends, and we had some very rummy casual lodgers. One of these men arrived with a frock coat and top hat and asked me to try them on, which I did. He put on my suit and suggested we should go to the theatre together. I foolishly agreed. During the performance I noticed that he had disappeared. Then I was approached by someone who asked me who I was. From what he said I gathered that my colleague was a wanted man. I quickly went back to the lodgings but found he had gone. So I lost my suit.

The book that I had now taken over was with a Friendly Society. In the normal way these books have to be bought, but I was a sub-agent. That is, I collected for the man who owned the book, and this meant that I was getting only part of the com-

nission. The business was in the slum area, and I certainly saw
uman nature in the raw there. This also applied to the type of
nsurance men with whom I came into contact, and I quickly fell
nto a gambling school again. This time it was mainly horse-racing.

In order to supplement our very meagre earnings it was
ustomary to collect for clothing clubs from the same customers.
Here I got an insight into a vicious system which I have never
orgotten. Even the place where we handed over our collections
vas depressing. To instil fear into the collectors as to what would
appen to them if they embezzled any money, the walls were
lastered with notices of convictions instituted and terms of
mprisonment imposed on collectors for this offence.

I was cured of betting on horses by two incidents. The first
s amusing in retrospect, but it was unpleasant when it happened.

I went to Lincoln Races for the first time. I had with me about
£1, and in the course of the afternoon I lost all but 2s. This I
lecided to put on the last race. There were only three runners,
nd the outsider was 6 to 1 against. However, I found a book-
naker offering 8 to 1 on the outsider, and I made my plunge with
im. To my surprise and pleasure, the horse came in first.

I had taken the precaution of standing near the bookie, and I
vas the first to hand in my ticket. He tore it up and asked me
o wait a minute as his clerk had gone away for some change. Very
uickly a queue of people formed behind me. When there was no
ign of the clerk returning, they began to get nasty, and eventually
nocked the bookie from his pedestal. To make matters worse, as
was so near, somebody took me for the clerk. I was knocked
over and only got out of the way by crawling underneath another
nan's stand. By this time it was a free fight, obviously engineered
by the bookie, who had disappeared in the clamour. All I got out
of it was grazed shins and torn trousers.

The other incident fortunately cured me completely. One day I
net one of these betting rogues in the street, and he told me that
e knew of a certainty. He suggested that he should put 5s on
his horse for me. Eventually I gave him the money and realised
fter we had parted that I'd forgotten to ask the name of the
orse. I went up to his lodgings at dinner time, but he had not

been back, and I knew that somewhere he was drinking my 5s away. When I found him later in the afternoon I heard, of course that the horse had lost. I realised how green I had been.

I came up against something even worse in connection with my insurance agency. The collection commission was a bare living and we depended mainly on commission paid for bringing in new business. If we persuaded someone to insure for 1s per week we were paid 12s, but if the business lapsed at any time before the first twelve weeks were up we had to repay it. It was easy enough to get business in very poor districts, but it was very difficult to keep it. The result was that I found I had received between £10 and £20 in commission, which I had spent, but had to repay it because the business turned out to be bad. I then made a decision not to introduce any more business of this sort but to repay the commission received and start afresh.

This meant that, after making allowance for repayments, I was left with only 7s a week. I lived on this for about four months until the whole amount was repaid. In order to do so I took a room at 3s 6d a week and lived on the other 3s 6d. I will not harass the reader by describing how to live on 3s 6d a week. Let it be enough to say that it was a gruelling experience, certainly not good for the constitution of a young man of my age. Still, the discipline had the effect of enabling me for the first time in my life to gain control of myself. I certainly knew what it was to be hungry during those months, and in later years I have had no difficulty, and have often found it beneficial, to fast for a day or so.

When I had cleared my obligations I was offered a job with a house purchase insurance company in Keighley at 25s a week.

I was then twenty. For the previous two years I had had a very rough time. I was apparently a failure both as a grocer and as an insurance agent. But at Keighley I made a decision which changed the whole course of my life and set me on the road to happiness and prosperity. Up to this time I had at no time paid more than 12s 6d a week for lodgings. Now I decided to find out something about 'the bettermos' sort of people' – to use my mother's phrase. So I took lodgings at 15s a week in a large terrace house occupied by a plumber and his wife, Mr and Mrs Jackson.

14
LEARNING TO ENJOY

> Sitting still and wishing
> Makes no person great.
> The Good Lord sends the fishing
> But you must dig the bait.

Up till this time I had not known what real happiness was, and my pleasures had been rather silly; but I had transgressed neither the moral nor the criminal code, perhaps through fear. I was ignorant of any form of culture. Nevertheless, I held strong opinions of many subjects, was narrow-minded, full of inhibitions and prejudices, and had still to develop a sense of humour. I had read nothing but the 1d novelettes, nor had I come into contact with anyone, apart from my schoolmasters, who read anything really worth while.

In my new lodgings I had a bedroom to myself for the first time in my life, and I shared a back sitting-room with the two other lodgers and George Jackson, the householder's son. One of the two lodgers was a Scot of about thirty-five, a self-educated man who had worked his way up in the business and who was, by the way, the first man I ever met who paid Income Tax, then 1s in the £1. Of this he complained bitterly. He possessed a Scot's sardonic sense of humour. The other lodger was a lady of about twenty-five, a health visitor, who was knowledgeable and sensible. George Jackson, who was then about twenty-two, was a solicitor's clerk and a local preacher. He was studying for the Wesleyan ministry. Hardworking and conscientious, he spent most of his time with his books in the front room.

My clumsy speech and lack of vocabulary made me shy of this coterie at first. But during meals, as I gained confidence, I began to express my mind on things I thought I knew about, and in no

uncertain terms. I have not forgotten standing on the hearthru
one night, holding forth in eloquent tones on some subject, an
saying, 'How anyone can think differently is absolutely beyon
my comprehension', and the Scotsman's reply, spoken ver
quietly: 'I can quite understand that.'

That sarcastic remark altered the course of my life. The ne
morning I said to George Jackson: 'I would like to know som
thing of the writers you talk about. Can you lend me some book
by Ruskin and Carlyle?' He said he could, but that he did n
think I should understand them. 'Are you interested in anythin
particular?' he asked. 'What about the book on clothes?'
replied. So he lent me *Sartor Resartus*.

I took this away and started to read it eagerly, but found that
could understand hardly a word of it. All the same, I doggedl
read it through, and found one or two sentences which seemed t
make sense. I then read it through again, with no better resul
so I took the book back to its owner and told him it was above m
He said that he had been thinking it over, and would recommen
that I should read first *Idle Thoughts of an Idle Fellow* by Jeron
K. Jerome.

This book by Jerome was the best thing I could possibly hav
read. It might have been written for me. It was about somethin
that I had experienced and could understand. For the first tim
in my life I laughed at myself and with myself. Reading this boo
aroused my dormant sense of humour, which has since been on
of my most valued assets. All the embarrassments I had suffere
such as being hard-up and having to pawn a watch, were n
longer degrading and depressing. I found that I had not only go
an insight into human nature by being hard-up, but was enjoyin
in retrospect a rich and amusing experience. The simple an
sound philosophy of this book, and of *Second Thoughts of an Id
Fellow,* which I read immediately afterwards, was something th
I could grasp and appreciate. The arguments swept away most o
my inhibitions. Reading them was like clearing the ground c
rubbish before starting to build on solid foundations. I have neve
read any book since that could have linked my illiterate mind s
effectively with literature.

Through the influence of George Jackson I joined the YMCA nd the Young Men's Class which was run by his church. In this ay I met many fine young men – apprentice engineers, moulders nd so on, several of whom I still count among my friends. Many f them had only about 6d a week pocket money. A series of ooklets called *The Penny Poets* was in great vogue, and many of ny early quotations were obtained from them. It was remarkable ow far 6d went in those days, if you didn't drink or smoke and hen you could buy the works of the classic poets for a 1d.

At the Young Mens' Class we had lectures, and I took part in lays and concerts. Through these social contacts I became mildly nterested in football and cricket for the first time. The YMCA as also a good social centre, and there in a debate I found myself uoting from *Sartor Resartus*. This surprised everybody, including nyself. Although I had read the book without much under-tanding, I could remember whole passages word for word.

On the strength of this supposed knowledge of the classics I vas made editor of the YMCA magazine. I did not like to admit hat what I had quoted was all I knew; but as my main job was to vrite an article each month, I took the risk.

My vocabulary, however, did not contain sufficient words for ne to express myself. I had to fight hard to find the right phrase. typical instance was when I wanted to stir members into eeping up their enthusiasm. We wanted not only 'starters', we vanted – I could not find the word. I had actually to take the para-raph to Bradford to ask a friend for it. The word was 'stickers'.

I commenced my private anthology by collecting words and hrases. I found whatever I wrote down I remembered, and if it vas worth making a note of it was worth referring to again. hrases, especially, I have always found useful. What other eople have said on any subject is usually so much better than vhat I could have said. So I took phrases from Carlyle, Ruskin nd Lowell, as well as Shakespeare, and they have provided me vith texts that effectively guided my conduct.

I also read weekly literature. One of my periodicals was *Great houghts,* which was then in vogue, though presently I found it vas inclined to be dead; but then I began to read *John O'London's*

Weekly, which was just what I needed as a gateway to literatur
Although I drifted away to some extent from my mould
friends at the Class, we still had a common interest in readin
this journal until it ceased publication.

Compared with young men who enjoy an all-round educatio
I had when young one or two advantages. Their knowledge
spread over many subjects not learned from choice but just as
means of passing examinations. I concentrated on one subjec
literature, with one clear objective, that of finding a way of lif
The idea was new and vital to me, and I was intense and en
thusiastic in my search. Whereas other young men found man
minor distractions, such as games, I lived in the country all m
boyhood, where I had little interest in sport and no speci
standards to maintain. My mind was as free and clear as a shallo
stream. I knew so little, that, if I read anything that appeared t
be a worthwhile truth, I wrote it down and accepted it as a part
life.

My first notes were from Carlyle, whom I cannot say I rea
with much understanding or a great deal of pleasure. I took ou
what I wanted and discarded the rest. Sometimes he gave me
text, and I preached the sermon to myself. Other passages I kept i
front of me to show me the way I should go. I placed them i
two different categories: Things to Do, and Things Not to Do
under the headings of 'Positive' and 'Negative'.

After a few months of life in my new environment at Keighley
I was a different person. I began to enjoy living; my circle
acquaintances was enlarging, my new interests developing. Bu
there was one disability which remained with me for many years
I still had traces of dialect in my speech, and this made me nervou
of meeting new people, especially in business. For a long time
could not pluck up courage to interview business men.

Strangely enough, for some time after I did not see again any
the three people who lived with me in Keighley. Then I discovere
the Scotsman set up in business for himself later and has sinc
died; the health visitor migrated to Canada, and George Jackso
became a minister. I always had in mind that I would like t
contact him and I was fortunate enough to do so. By that tim

e was a Wesleyan minister, had a charming wife and a fine family
f four sons, who have all had a university education and are
aking their mark in the world.

On my twenty-first birthday I received a letter from a girl who
ad been a friend of mine at school. She reminded me that at the
ge of ten or eleven I had prophesied that I would be worth a
illion pounds at the age of twenty-one. She wanted to know if
had achieved my ambition. This gave me a shock, for at the
me my cash in hand was under £1. It was obvious something
ad gone wrong with my programme. I decided to find out what
was.

For this purpose I adopted an unusual method. At that time I
as studying business literature and balance sheets in particular.
had been reading a report of an investigation into a company's
fairs, and this gave me the idea to make an inventory of myself,
find out the cause of my failure and to estimate my real worth.
drew up a report and balance sheet of my life and listed my
ock-in-trade, faithfully recording my virtues and vices.

This was illuminating. I found few positive virtues and many
eaknesses, but it was consoling to feel that many of the vices
ere merely negative. For instance, two of my weaknesses were
anity and sentimentality; but I found no trace of jealousy or
nvy, which seem to absorb so much of many people's lives.

Besides making a full survey and preparing a balance sheet for
y private information, I drafted a more general report which I
ddressed to all interested parties, including my correspondent. I
pent a lot of time on this. It was my first attempt at writing
nything out of the ordinary, and while it may appear somewhat
rude, at that time it gave me some amusement and no little
atisfaction. It ran as follows:

Dear Shareholder in the concern of my life, You wish to know the state of my affairs. I have therefore conducted an inquiry into the business and herewith present my report.

The firm was established in 1890, the founders being an agricultural worker and his wife, who had created six other similar sound, going concerns. To begin with, this subsidiary offspring was constitutionally sound. The trading in the early days was the usual mixed type, and was mainly concerned with matters of health, religion and economy. The business developed normally for the first thirteen years, after which I was given complete control, the founders retaining only a debenture interest.

Up to this point all was well, but I regret to record that with the change of management the character of the business deteriorated and weaknesses began to show themselves. In seeking for new ventures offering quicker and easier profits, the bread and butter side of the business was neglected, while the religious section was declared redundant on the grounds that it was a long-term investment, that the competition was too keen and immediate profits too small. Several speculative lines were tried, but all failed.

Consequently, for the last few years the concern has barely been kept alive. The only additional asset which seems to have been acquired during this period is a small knowledge of human nature which has been bought dearly, though there are signs that it may eventually prove of considerable value.

So much for the past. Fortunately the future looks brighter. After seven years in the wilderness the concern has suddenly taken a new lease of life. A reorganisation is taking place, and bad stock is being sorted out. When this has been completed it is hoped that confidence in the undertaking will be restored. The inquiry shows the business to be fundamentally sound but short of saleable stock. However, fresh capital is being attracted to the business, and actually negotiations are at present in progress for a partnership or merger with a very enterprising Yorkshire firm with good connections in the original line of business.

If this takes place the name and the style of the business will remain unaltered, but it may mean my relinquishing the position of Managing Director. At the same time it is felt that the amalgamation should do much to strengthen and vitalise the business. Taking into account certain hidden assets and underdeveloped resources, I feel the shares are undervalued at the present time, and I confidently advise the few remaining shareholders not to sell, but to wait for capital appreciation.

Optimistically yours.

After ninety years trading in the business of life a million pounds ill eludes me, but I can say that I would not exchange my ccumulated assets – which I cannot measure in cash – for that sum.

The self-analysis was my most important landmark up to wenty-one. Till then it was almost as though my mind had been vacuum. I had never been conscious of what I was doing or what could do. My decisions, such as they were, had been made from ecessity. For the first time I understood something about yself. I seemed to wake up to find that I did have some capital use.

What consoled me was that, in spite of some dissipation of my ssets, I was still solvent, physically and mentally. I had already iscarded many petty vices and some of the inhibitions that had ngled my life. In drawing up this statement I treated it in much e same way as a school report, going through all the subjects to nd what interested me most and how I could improve myself.

I did not attempt at this stage to map out my entire future life ut rather to improve my immediate prospects. At that time I was orking for a third-rate insurance company, in which I did not ave a lot of confidence. Therefore I decided to make a change.

Through my association with the YMCA I had got to know the anager of a small but sound insurance company whose business as mainly with Quakers. He offered me a position as an inspector Leeds at £3 a week, and this I accepted. After my experiences in eighley I began to appreciate how much social status depended n superior lodgings, and I now aspired to an apartment.

I arranged to share a sitting-room with a young man, just down rom Oxford, who had obtained an executive position with a soap rm. It was a large, old-fashioned house occupied by two maiden dies who had seen better days. They were very prim and proper, ut never tired of mentioning their own one indiscretion. pparently when they were young girls, they played truant and ent to a fair. With all the abandon of youth they let themselves o and went on the swings, roundabouts and even into the ideshows. Finally, they bought some oranges and went behind a tall to eat them. 'We didn't care', they said.

At first I had little in common with my room-companion. He

had obviously lived in another world, part of which he ha
brought with him in the shape of his own large Oxford diva
basket chair, padded with cushions. These chairs were ver
fashionable at the time. How I envied him! He was fond o
poetry, and I did not understand it. One day he was readin
something which amused him very much, and at intervals h
burst out laughing. This was something new to me. I had neve
heard of poetry making people laugh, and I asked him what it wa
about. He read some verses out to me. It was from one of Charle
Stuart Calverley's parodies:

> Can'st thou love me, lady,
> I've not learnt to woo.
> Thou art on the shady side of sixty too.
>
> Still I love thee dearly,
> Thou hast lands and pelf,
> But I love thee merely, merely for thyself.
>
> I am plain but then,
> Thou, to speak sincerely,
> Art as plain again.

I was enchanted. This was my weight. I immediately went to
bookshop and brought a paperback copy of Calverley's works, an
in a short time I knew several of them by heart. 'Gemini and C
Virgo' particularly appealed to me as I had had a similar experienc
when a boy at school. Another favourite was 'Cuckoo'. Apa
from its humour and romantic appeal, it still brings to my min
the atmosphere of the cuckoo season.

I have never been able to appreciate highbrow or moder
poetry, but humorous and light verse has fascinated me ever sinc
I started to discover humorous poetry after this, and one versifie
whom I particularly liked was Harry Graham.

While I was now getting much more enjoyment from my soci
life, I was by no means out of the wood so far as business wa
concerned. The firm I was working for did all classes of insuranc
business and, whereas by this time I knew something of li
insurance, I knew nothing about the fire and general business

as also expected to transact. Our clients were nice people, but ey did expect me to know my job. Then there were very big gaps my social make-up. For instance up to that time I had never oken on the telephone, nor had I come in contact with educated eople. I had an inferiority complex and dreaded meeting anyone, nd as a matter of fact did everything I could to avoid interviews.

After much mental anguish I sent in my resignation at the end f six months, saying that I found I had not sufficient training to do e job properly. To my surprise the manager came to see me and ressed me to stay, and the company were so concerned that they ent one of the managers from head office to see if he could per-uade me. They said they were quite satisfied with what I could do, nd that wider knowledge would come to me with patience.

However, I had come to the conclusion that I had tried to move o fast. I thought I now knew better what I could really do. I vas much interested in a new type of insurance then being intro-uced. There was a vast difference between the benefits derived rom life assurance on premiums paid weekly and yearly. In the atter case it was an investment out of which you not only had the enefit of the insurance, but had your money back with interest at he end of a period. In the weekly business more than half the remium went in expenses, and the public got very poor value or their money.

The larger industrial companies transacting weekly business vere now beginning to offer monthly policies embracing all the dvantages of the endowment business. So I took an agency with leading insurance company to develop this business. Although ny ordinary wage was only about 30s I was able to make £4 a veek including commission, which was even more than the early business would have paid me. Industrial agents were rather oath to undertake this monthly business, the commission being o much smaller, but in view of my experience I was asked to give lecture showing how much easier it was to earn bigger money vith smaller commission. To my surprise I was afterwards treated s something of an authority on the subject.

15
FIRST WORLD WAR AND MARRIAGE

If you get a prudent, healthy wife, your industry, in your profession, with her good economy, will be fortune sufficient.

BENJAMIN FRANKLIN

I clearly remember the first time I met the girl I was destined t marry. It was in 1912 when I was twenty-two years old. I ha recently come to Bradford and was taking a stroll in Manninghar Park one day, when I noticed two girls sitting on a seat.

One of the girls I knew slightly, her name was Rose. Sh introduced me to her friend May, adding impressively 'my boss At that moment Rose's boy friend arrived on the scene and I wa invited to join them at the park café. As it had always been m ambition to be my own boss, I was intrigued by the description c May as 'the boss', and I was glad to accept the invitation. Here, i seemed, was a chance to find out how it was done.

However I discovered that while the description of 'boss' wa correct, her position was not quite as glamorous as the titl suggested. May, who was then aged eighteen, explained that sh was a working partner in a small family business in the market She earned £2 a week, while I was only earning 35s. Her wealt at that time consisted of a three-speed bicycle, mine was an Inger soll watch, value 5s, and a rolled gold chain worth 1s 6d. Regula meetings with May now followed and indeed I was to be seein her for the next fifty-four years.

May was the youngest of twelve children. Her mother, Mr Baxandall, was by any measure a remarkable woman. Her fathe had been a dyer's labourer in early life, but lost his job throug eavy drinking and ended up as a debt collector. Although he was ill alive when I met the family, I never saw him and his name as not mentioned even when he died shortly afterwards. And hen, later in life, my wife discovered I enjoyed a drink of lager, ie was quite distressed. I had not been able to afford it when we ere courting. Eventually she overcame her distrust and learned enjoy it too.

The explanation of how Mrs Baxandall brought up twelve ildren is unknown. No doubt the boys, as they left school, ould contribute to the family budget. When she was fifty-seven, nly three of her daughters remained at school and Mrs Baxandall ecided to go into business.

She took a stall in Bradford market with the slogan, used in iose days, of 'Nothing above a Penny'. Indeed, her capital could ot have been more than a pound or two, but I suppose the orkshire motto 'Nowt from nowt leaves nowt' had some ifluence on the early part of the business.

It was based on a small profit margin. Credit was not allowed, id if a customer was interested in a hat at 3s 11d, she was not ersuaded to buy one at 4s 6d. It succeeded to the extent that, hen the first sister left school, Mrs Baxandall was able to take her n as an assistant. The next two girls were also found jobs and hen I first met May, her mother rented three stalls which they alled shops. They had by this time expanded from the 'penny' ito the millinery business, and next to the hat stall they rented stall for flowers. These appealed to customers seeking flowers nd hats for funerals who were able to pay ready cash out of isurance money.

After their mother died seven years later, the business continued expand. Yet another trader, this time in furs, was bought out nd shops outside the market were acquired, one of which sold nly buttons.

Their next project was to open a cafe in the market, which roved most popular. A typical menu provided sausage, chips nd peas for 1s 3d. Tea and cakes cost 6d.

During business hours I was never allowed to see May. These vere from 9am to 10pm on Saturdays and from 9am to 7pm

during the week. We made up for these restrictions on Wednesda
half-closing day, when we went on some excursion or other.

In the glorious summer of 1914, we went on our first holida
together at Blackpool. May's mother opposed the idea, on
relenting when I bought an engagement ring. It was a sing
diamond and cost £13 10s. Instructions were issued to th
landlady that we were not to sleep in the same part of the hous
and could only communicate by messages. The price of eac
bedroom was 3s (15p today) and this included any cooking w
needed. We made the most of every day, getting up at 6.30 an
going for a long walk before breakfast. On our return to Bradfor
the First World War had already started.

May's family had a different outlook from mine on certai
aspects of social behaviour. An example of this was on th
occasion of May's twenty-first birthday, when I bought a gift an
presented it later in the day. Apparently she had expected
birthday card from me, but none had arrived. I explained t
Mrs Baxandall that it was not customary in my family to sen
birthday cards. She said: 'You must always remember you ar
living in a civilised country.'

On one of my visits to May's house, I noticed a difference in th
furniture. The cushions of the sofa and chairs were bulging a
odd angles. 'Whatever has been used to stuff these?' I aske
'It seems like paper.' It was. The explanation was simple. The
were packed tight with bank notes.

All the family were members of the Yorkshire Penny Bank
but as this was solely for a savings account, another bank wa
needed to provide cheque books necessary for business. On on
occasion, when May presented the week-end's takings at th
bank, the counter clerk said: 'My word, you had a good day o
Saturday.' On hearing this, Mrs Baxandall immediately closed th
account and crammed the takings into cushions until anothe
bank was selected for their business account.

At the beginning of the 1914 war, one of May's sisters ha
already married and another married shortly afterwards. Mr
Baxandall gave each of them a house and most of the furnitur
they needed. Their husbands had enlisted at the beginning of th

'ar and I joined what was known as the Derby Scheme. This ɪeant I could wear an armlet to show I had enlisted, but was not et due for calling up.

People were not so war-conscious then as in 1939. Like most ɔung men, I thought that fighting was the job of the professional ɔldiers, a race apart. Except for George Brown, I had not come ɪto contact with a soldier, and certainly had never known anyone 'ho became a casualty.

Only after the regular army was wiped out by the end of 1914 id I begin to realise that I might be involved. An attack of eritonitis, involving a big operation, weakened my constitution, ɔ that when eventually I was called up in 1916, I was relegated ɔ the Pay Corps. Frankly, I considered myself lucky to be out of a ghting unit.

My period of service was quite without glory and I can only laim I did a useful job when the chance came my way. After ɪort spells in one or two branches of Army accountancy, I found ɪy ideal billet. All casualties, payments, and so on, were typed on lips for subsequent costing against the individual soldier's ccount. Many errors found their way into these slips, and it eeded imagination to sort them out. This happened to come asily to me, and in due course I organised a department and :ained staff to deal with this finicky business. This rendered me ɪdispensable and the powers that be left me alone.

When I was originally called up it was October 1916 and we had rranged to get married in December, so it was very much a war ɪarriage. I was due to go on furlough for Christmas and had pplied to go a week earlier so I could be married. But two days efore the date we had arranged, my application was turned down nd we had to call it off. And then, at four o'clock on the afternoon f the day before we had planned to marry, my pass was suddenly ranted.

I rushed to my lodging, put on a new uniform coat and found, ʋhen I got to the train, that it belonged to a much taller man than ɪyself and twice as large. When I arrived in Bradford to say the ʋedding was on again, it was too late to make any arrangements. ſoreover, it was the Christmas season and a busy time for my wife's family, so we had neither guests nor friends to act a witnesses.

It was a frosty morning and the church was on top of a hil I stayed overnight in Bradford and went to church by tram whic got stuck in the snow, so I had to walk the last half mile. My bric was equally unfortunate, her taxi could not climb the hill and sh had to walk, arriving twenty minutes late. By this time the vica and I had concluded the formalities, but as May was by hersel the ceremony was again delayed until the sexton fetched h sister from a nearby mill to act as a witness. She sobbed througl out the service, which added a final touch of melancholy to th proceedings. Military marriages in those dark days were mad often before a soldier went to the front line; they were ofte tragically short. In spite of the depressing start, however, ou turned out very happily.

After the ceremony, we walked down the hill to May's mother' house. Her mother lay ill in bed and called out: 'Don't come up The only thing to eat is some cold rice pudding in the larder.' Bu we had to forego this wedding feast in order to catch the train fo Blackpool, which we just managed to do.

The honeymoon over, we started our married life in a fla attached to a shop owned by my mother-in-law. It had not bee occupied for some time, and at night we were often disturbed b rats running over the bed.

As I had been posted to York, I bought a Raleigh three-spee bicycle for £5 so that I could cycle the thirty-five miles from Yor to Bradford when I was lucky enough to get leave, which wa most week-ends.

In between, my wife lived with her mother and continued t work in the market. Financially she was better off than I was whe we were first married. She had £200 capital and I had £160.

Our first child, a daughter, was born about the time of th Armistice. Unfortunately I was not allowed to see her as I' contracted the deadly influenza which was then sweepin England, leaving a high mortality rate.

Yorkshire caution would manifest itself from time to time in m wife's character. We always kept our business finances separat and long after we were married, when I wished to borrow a sum from her for a short period, she laughed and said: 'I wouldn't lend you a penny. I'm keeping mine for when you go bankrupt.' The reason for this was that mine was a speculative business and she wanted to be sure there was ample cash set aside should things go wrong.

Even when we prospered sufficiently to travel to faraway places May would book an economy ticket on the same plane as I was travelling first. Arriving at Barbados on one occasion, she said: 'There you see, I've got here as soon as you and saved £200.' After we came to live in Morecambe and had to travel to Bradford, when the first-class fare increased from 18s to £1, May immediately went second class.

Her sound business acumen and financial independence were invaluable to me, as I could then afford to take a calculated risk from time to time.

The Baxandalls were a close-knit family, especially the three sisters, who not only worked together in the market, but for eighteen years lived in adjacent houses, and, curiously enough, each one died at the age of seventy-three.

May was the last survivor. She had enjoyed excellent health until six months before she died, when unfortunately she developed cancer. When she became seriously ill, it was necessary to dispose of the business assets. This was done in bits and pieces, first the outside shops and then the cafe. Seven days before she died, only the millinery remained unsold. There was a lot of competition, but May refused to sell to anyone associated with the credit business.

At last came a man who was prepared to sell his credit business to comply with her wishes. At the interview she said: 'Promise me across your heart, you will never sell anything on credit under the Baxandall name.' This he promised. And from recent enquiries I made, this promise has been honoured.

Although May was a typical Yorkshire lass, in that she always took care of the pennies, she was, at the same time, very generous. In the few days before she died, May sent cheques to each of the fourteen remaining members of her staff in the market.

We had a happy married life; both of us were fond of travel and were lucky enough to visit most of the pleasant places in the world. For the last ten years of our life together, we wintered in the West Indies.

We have a son and daughter who have never given us a moment's worry and the family now consists of eight grandchildren and six great-grandchildren.

When I was demobilised early in 1919 I was, like a good many other young men both in that war and the next, very unsettled. I noticed in particular at the end of the Second World War that in cases of young men who had entered the Army after being, say, shop assistants or apprentices, they were often promoted to commissioned rank and held down important positions. When they came out again they found themselves having to start from scratch once more. As Butler says: 'People are like cows. When they enter a strange field, they immediately walk round to find if there is any way in which they can break through, or a way out, and if they cannot find any, they settle down and graze contentedly'.

My own position in 1919 was that insurance and grocery were the only businesses I knew anything about. I had never been good at either and wanted a change. Perhaps it was inevitable that in my first post-war venture I lost nearly all my capital. My idea was to set up as an insurance broker. As a side line, I bought a greengrocery business for £1,000, by putting down a deposit of £100 and arranging a mortgage for the balance. I intended to put in as manager a young man whom I knew and who knew something about the trade. I felt I was capable of supervising it.

Before engaging the young man, however, I thought I would learn something about buying. I got up at half-past four the first morning and went to the wholesale market. After being there an hour I realised my mistake.

Far more knowledge was required than I had imagined. I had gone too far to withdraw from the purchase, but after serious consideration, I decided not to appoint my friend but to see if I could resell the business. Fortunately, there was quite a boom at the time, and I had no difficulty in realising a £50 profit, but I was hocked to learn that the costs of the transaction were something ike £70. So that little bit of experience cost me £20.

Perhaps I had not very much justification for setting up on my own as an insurance broker, but I felt I should be a freelance, and hat it was better to be at the head of a mouse than at the tail of n elephant. I took a small office and was doing reasonably well n the brokerage business when a small incident changed the ourse of my whole life again and set me on the road to prosperity.

One day a taxi-driver came to see me. He wanted to know if I vould advertise his house for sale, as he did not want his clients o know he was leaving. If it was sold, he would pay me the ıormal commission. I knew something about property through ny experience with the house purchase company, but I had never ttempted to sell a house. However, I said I would try. It was large terrace house, and he wanted £1,000 for it. I thought that vas a lot, but we were in the boom period of 1919, and an dvertisement was duly framed.

The following morning to my surprise two men were waiting vhen I arrived at the office, and they were arguing about who had een there first. Both had come to buy the house. I said the rgument could soon be settled – had either of them brought the £100 deposit? One had, and he won. I remembered enough bout property transactions to know that in order to conclude he matter a contract must be signed. Since I had no idea how to vord such a document, I rang up a friend who had been in the state business. He said he had an old contract form, which he vould send round. I filled this in, and the prospective purchaser, vho had not stopped to question the price, asked if he could read he contract over to his solicitor on the telephone.

I agreed, but I was on tenterhooks. The solicitor objected to one clause in the contract, and said he must see the abstract of itle. All this was double Dutch to me, but I was determined, ıaving got so near, to get the contract signed if I could. So I asked he man if he would excuse me. Then I went into the office next loor and rang up the only solicitor I knew to ask him if there vas any way out of the dilemma. He said: 'Offer to give him a narketable title.' I changed the clause and, though I had no idea

what the wording meant, to my infinite relief it was agreed to by
the purchaser's solicitor. £100 in notes was paid over.

It was only after the buyer had left that I dared to think abou
the commission. I rang up my ex-estate agent friend again and
asked him what the correct charge was. He told me 2 per cent – in
other words £20. It seemed too good to be true. I had neve
before earned so much money so easily or so quickly.

By the time the taxi-driver came I was wondering if I dare ask
£5. However, when I told him I had sold it for the price he had
asked, he was obviously pleased. When I added that I had go
£100 deposit and that the usual commission was £20 he said a
once that I could deduct that amount.

Without any hesitation I decided to become an estate agent
During the rest of the morning I made my plans and at lunch I
told my wife. I said I thought the £20 commission would serve
for capital if she could manage without household expenses fo
three months. I knew my small office up three flights of stairs
would be of no use for an estate agent's business, so I gave a
month's notice, looked round for something more suitable, and
duly found it with an old-fashioned firm of tailors who had a corne
suite of rooms on the second floor let on a yearly tenancy, at the
low rent of £65, to a firm who were moving to ground-floor
premises.

During the month I spent looking for offices I was also learning
something about selling property on commission. It was very
much a seller's market at that period, and the difficulty was
finding houses to sell. But people usually waited for something
they wanted to be advertised. I soon collected a list of people
wanting homes and took the risk of advertising on their behalf
In this way I started selling before I went into my offices. I was
dealing mainly with small houses, and I did not concern mysel
unduly with my own profits. I was learning and paying my way
and it was a pleasure to give all the service I could. What did
surprise me was how people responded to my assistance or any
small financial concession I made. One recommended another
and very often the buyer would give me his own house to sell
In this way I might have had a run of five or six sales from selling

ne house initially. The press was my shop window, and I decided
› spend half of my gross profits on advertising.

Very soon, apart from my small advertisements, I began taking
half-page in the local newspaper once a week at £50 a time.
ome of this advertising was rather crude, but it worked. I was in
igh spirits. I had plenty of energy and initiative and looking back,
ıy view is that an ounce of initiative in a young business is worth
ton of capital. Whatever success I have had since then has been
ue to moves initiated in those first two or three years.

My idea about advertising was that it should be readable and
ıtertaining, but never misleading. Being responsible for the
ɔst of advertising made me very careful what properties I offered
ɔr sale. I inspected every one and only accepted those for sale
hich were offered at the proper market price. I was now getting
lot of fun out of life, and I collected humorous quotations for
se in my advertising. One I remember:

> Midst pleasures and palaces,
> Wherever you may roam,
> You just provide the little bride
> And we provide the home.

Another started on a more serious note; 'New times demand
ew measures and new men,' and I went on to write about
ɔssilised firms and old-fashioned methods of transacting business.
'he next morning the landlord of the office came up to see me.
Ie was white with anger. He said I would have to leave. People
ere saying this advertisement was intended to make him a
.ughing stock. I had no thought of him when framing the
dvertisement, though it certainly did apply in his case. However,
e calmed down when I explained that I was referring only to
state agents.

About this time I helped to found the Publicity Club in
radford. We used to have interesting and amusing lectures on
ublicity and enjoyed discussing common problems. One lecture
remember was on 'prestige' advertising. The advertising
ıanager of Jowett Cars asked the lecturer his opinion of a
articular advertisement Jowett's were then running. It depicted

a new Jowett car standing at the gate of an old castle with bright young girl stepping into it. The caption underneath ra 'Ancient and Modern', and in order to test the pulling power the advertisement they had inserted on the number plate, C.9 He said it was surprising how many people had looked up No 9 in *Hymns Ancient and Modern* and how many parsons had writte complaining they were being irreverent, for the first line of th hymn began: 'Ride on, ride on, in majesty.' The lecturer replie that he didn't think much of the advertisement in any case, but h couldn't understand why people should think C.99 referred t *Ancient and Modern*. If he himself had been sufficiently influence he would have looked up Chant 99, the opening words of whic he thought began: 'Put not thy trust in chariot wheels.'

I always had a feeling that my own advertising matter wa amateurish and on one occasion, when I was feeling lazy, thought I would engage a professional advertising firm, for change, to draw up a rather large advertisement. I explained m requirements to a young man from one of the local advertisin firms and suggested that he should draw up a draft for me to se When I saw his attempt, I was surprised to see how little he ha been able to grasp what I had in mind. I thought the appeal in h advertisement was not specific enough.

I told him so, and he promised to let me have another draft th next morning. The same night I prepared some notes myself c the type of advertisement I wanted. I took this along to the offi next morning and, after seeing his second attempt, I suggested t him that he should have a look at mine; there might be one or tw ideas in it which he could incorporate in his own. I saw him at th end of an hour and found that he had done nothing. He explaine that having read my draft through he could not alter a word of i

This story is no reflection on advertising agents. The moral that a man writing advertisements for any firm must live insic the firm. The advertisement I devised, by the way, was one of th most successful I ever had.

16
DEALING IN PROPERTY

I have heard of a man who had a mind to sell his house, and therefore carried a piece of brick in his pocket, which he shewed as a pattern to encourage purchases.

JONATHAN SWIFT

cannot expect the average reader to be interested in the technical-ies of the property business, but it may be useful if I state some f the principles I applied in this new venture of mine and indicate ow, from fairly small beginnings, the business I founded in my oung manhood became one of the largest of its kind in the ountry.

At first my business consisted of selling houses on commission. 'hese were mostly small vacant houses. The immediate prospects ere promising. It was simple for me under the conditions then btaining to sell four or five houses each week. I realised, how-ver, that the boom would not last for ever, and that I must build omething more permanent out of the nucleus I had created.

There were two ways of expanding. I could develop a legitimate state agency practice, or I could use my slender capital to buy nd sell property. I saw that eventually these two projects ould not be able to run together, but I decided to experiment ith both for a year. I had picked up a good knowledge of roperty management, but I was not qualified to make valuations nd do many other jobs that required technical training. So I ook the risk of appointing a young man who had recently ualified both as surveyor and estate agent. At the same time I ought my first block of property. I had noticed that the houses milar to those I was selling with vacant possession for, say, '500, realised only half that price when sold in blocks, the reason eing that the investment income was poor because of low rents

and the tenant's protection by the Rent Restriction Act of 191
It seemed to me a simple thing to buy wholesale and sell to th
tenant, with a small deposit and a mortgage for the balance, whic
could then be repaid for a shilling or two more than the weekl
rent. This gave the tenant two advantages. Over a period of yea
the house would be paid for or, if he wanted to sell in the mear
time, he could make a substantial profit. I found there were tw
main reasons why tenants did not buy. The houses were often i
poor repair and if the tenant became the owner, he would b
responsible for upkeep. Also, landlords usually expected tenant
to pay something in the region of the vacant possession pric
I decided to get all the necessary repairs done before offering th
houses for sale and to limit my profit to £25 a house. I ha
always wanted to put into practice the slogan on the grocery va
when I started to work, 'Small Profits and Quick Returns'; and
had not failed to notice the success of the Woolworth systen
based on the same principle.

I may have been responsible for an important change in th
housing policy of Bradford. On walking down to business, I sa
a notice outside a large block of terrace houses – sizeable house
with lawns in front. The notice read: 'Offers for No. 3.' The offe
had to be in before a certain date. I knew the people who live
there were hard up, so I put in an offer for £500. This wa
accepted.

I then had to decide what to do with the property and decide
to turn it into flats. I did not then know that any type of flat wa
prohibited in Bradford because the Medical Officer of Healt
for the town was on the Housing Committee and claimed tha
converted flats were unhealthy. On collecting information,
discovered that thousands of pounds were lost in rates throug
houses standing empty. I carefully pointed this out when I mad
my application again and this time it was accepted. I converte
the house into three flats which proved readily saleable, and soo
the whole terrace was converted.

At the end of my first year in the property business my person
balance sheets made very satisfactory reading. I had saved fa
more than I had ever earned previously in one year. I had learr

lot about the estate business, and I had begun to get more out
: life. In the words of Swift: 'Business was my pleasure and my
easure business.'

One thing was essential – the small profit margin did not allow
r the occasional wrong deal, so I had to buy wisely. One mistake
the early stages would have tied up my small capital and put me
it of business. I had one or two near-misses through buying
ieap property below the owner-occupier standard, possibly not
ceptable as mortgage security. At the same time, with the idea
: spreading the risk, I formed a small company. This was
iccessful, but the capital available was little more than I could
ive commanded myself. Moreover, I was so afraid of losing
ther people's money that in doubtful buys I took the risk myself
id only passed to the company deals I was more or less sure about.

Much of my buying was done in the auction room. I had one
rly lesson which cured me of having anything to do with rings
r arrangements. In Bradford there were two or three competitors
iying the same types of property as myself, and I was often asked
stand in but refused. On one occasion there were two lots for
le, and there appeared to be only two likely buyers present –
iother competitor and myself. I fell for his suggestion that we
iould not outbid each other. He would bid for the first lot and
and down for the second. He bought the first lot much below the
rice I should have given. When my turn came there was outside
ompetition, which sent the price higher than I could afford to pay.

While I made £25 profit per house my limit, I very often
cepted less for quick sales. On one occasion I bought sixteen
ottages for £164 each. One of the occupiers came to see me after
ie auction and said that eight tenants were there and willing to
iy at £185. I told him that if he could persuade *all* the sixteen to
iy they could have them at £180 each. They all signed contracts
iat night.

It was not long before most of this class of property in Bradford
id district was absorbed, and I turned my attention to other
eas. Such, however, were my beginnings in a fascinating
here of activity.

I recall a letter I received from a Bradford man, Albert

Swindlehurst, written in a beautiful copperplate with curlicues. had offered him a house in Victoria Street which he was willing t consider, as his present house was infested with vermin. H wrote:

> Perhaps you are not aware that Oliver Goldsmith was a authority on bugs. Female bugs, he tells you, lay 150 eggs eac two days after impregnation, so in warm weather a few becom a lot, to put it mildly! Old bugs can, of course, be killed by co fumes, but I have seen eggs in thousands looking like bunch of microscopic pearly ovals, hanging like grapes in transpare bunches. Now, it is these that cause the trouble, neither hot n cold destroys their latent vitality. They may lie months befo the conditions for hatching are favourable. Then the ban begins to play again. In houses where they have been allowe to roam and infect furniture, they thrive until at last they a master.
>
> When the tenants leave and the house becomes cold, the nest away for warmth and multiply by eating each other. Hen the difficulty of extermination.

He continued in his letter:

> Fleas soon get out of their way for they love a fat flea . . You will think this a curious business epistle, but there wan a lot more romance in business life today. It has become col blooded and uninteresting to those of a more sentimental tur

Would Mr Swindlehurst have considered the following ane dote romantic? There were back-to-back houses where most the working class lived. The poorer type had a living-roo cellar-head and two bedrooms, with a wc for every two house The better type had a living-room, scullery, two bedrooms and separate wc immediately outside. These were much in dema as they were mortgageable.

In all cases of dispute the rent collector was the arbiter. On o occasion the occupant of a front house had a bonfire of old pape which showered out of the chimney onto the washing hangi on the line of her neighbour in the rear house. This so incens he neighbour that when it was the turn of the occupants of the ront house to use the wc she put a rim of tar round the seat. Jnwittingly the woman from the front house sat on this and in urn was furious. Her husband offered to placate her by wiping : off her backside. 'Wipe it off?' she cried indignantly. 'You'll not ouch that till the rent collector's seen it.'

There was one occasion in my early business days when it ecame necessary to enlarge my staff and it gave me an amusing nstructive experience. I had, and still have, a great admiration or Scotsmen. I had noticed that Scotsmen always seem to do well n England and carry more prestige than their English counter-arts. There is something in the old story about a Scotsman who ent his son to England to visit various businesses. On his return e was asked what he thought of the English. He replied that nfortunately he had not met any as he had been dealing only vith the heads of departments. My experience is that this young nan was rather slow. If he had contacted the owners of the usiness, rather than the departmental heads, he would have ound that they were invariably Englishmen.

For my part, I thought at the time that a Scotsman would be a seful addition and add a little prestige to my firm. I advertised n a Scottish paper and in due course went to Glasgow to interview he applicants. They were all fully qualified men, but for once I ad to confess that I could not size them up. I expected them to be our, but in addition I found them to be dumb. However, I ppointed the man I thought to be the likeliest applicant, but took he precaution of making it a six months' trial.

He turned out to be a complete failure, and within a month I new the reason why. He still retained all his native characteristics nd had made no attempt to acclimatise himself to English onditions. I had made the mistake of going over the border to empt a man out of his environment. I should have advertised in n English paper. Then, if a Scotsman had walked over the order on his own account, he would have been prepared to adapt imself. I tried this method immediately afterwards and engaged nother Scotsman who was a great success.

One of my earliest deals involved buying sixteen houses for

£95 each in St Stephen's Road, Bradford. One of these I sold wit vacant possession for £200, the rest at £135, arranging a mortgag with a building society of £120 for each tenant. For those unabl to meet the difference, I arranged a second mortgage for which made myself responsible. This meant there was little more fc them to pay than they had previously been paying in rent.

Not every tenant understood the implications, and a tenar arrived at my office one day and handed me the keys of her house 'Well, I'm leaving now', she said. 'And thank you very much When I explained that the house was hers and she could now se it and make a profit she replied. 'I'll leave it with you.' I was abl to get £350 for the house and she invested the money in a tax business for her son.

As news of this and other sales spread, there was less difficult in persuading tenants to buy on a mortgage. I had no idea at th time that this speculation began a movement to encourage th lower income groups to become house owners instead o tenants.

At this stage I began to realise the importance of finance i property dealings, as at the beginning I had had no credit facilitie and my transactions had been limited to my own cash reserves This meant much wasted time and opportunity, as I had to sel each lot before I could buy again. The right properties are no always on hand, and sometimes when I had the cash available was tempted to buy below the standard required for my purpose only to find that money was tied up when a better propositio became available. Experience has taught me there are thre essentials to property dealing: knowledge, money and patience and the last is by no means the least. Although the capital of th company remained small, we eventually had considerable collatera resources and banking facilities to enable dealing on a mucl larger scale.

Some time before, I had been experimenting in buying small lot in London, but after the company was formed I now looked rounc for larger estates and in due course the opportunity came along tc acquire an estate of 300 better-class artisan houses, which we pur chased for £65,000. This lot was in two parts, one in Soutl ondon and one in East London. At that particular time East ondon estates were not popular with either property owners or uilding societies, since they were among the first to come under ocialist-controlled councils and in consequence the rates were ery high. In my innocence I ignored this consideration in my aluation of the property. However, it turned out well because all ne tenants were working-class people of a good type. We have a aying in Yorkshire; 'There's nowt wrong wi' reet folk', and nis certainly applied in their case.

There was an amusing incident in the negotiations with the wner of the estate. It was my biggest purchase up to that time, nd I was feeling the strain of tackling this astute property man by nyself. We started our negotiations at noon and it was four hours ater before they were concluded. In the meantime, I knew, there were one or two people waiting outside who also wanted to buy.

The owner was a gentleman of the old school, who went very neticulously into every detail. It was a mixed bag I was buying, ncluding houses, shops, ground rents and a building repair usiness. He insisted on writing out every detail of the agreement, uring which we had various small differences of opinion. Finally e lifted his pen and said: 'Did you expect to include the builder's ard?' I had completely forgotten about this, but said: 'Yes, of ourse.' He took the paper in his hand to tear it up, then suddenly hanged his mind and said: 'I didn't, but I'll give you the damned ning.'

Before this deal, when I first started to buy property on my own n London, I was young and inexperienced. I was buying only in mall lots, and I carefully vetted most of the tenants. One of them ad told me he had seen a vacant house at Erith that he wanted to uy, but the owners would sell only eight, and he thought it night be worth my while to buy them and sell him the one he vanted. I went over to negotiate with the agent, but could get no atisfaction, so I got to know the name of the owner and wrote to im. I said I was interested in purchasing some property in Erith nd would like to meet him. To my surprise I received a letter nviting me to meet him for lunch at the Savoy. I thought this was ather odd, but it was a new experience for me, and I made up my mind that, however good the lunch might be, I would not let affect my price.

When I arrived at the Savoy I was introduced to the owner b the porter. He said he would not discuss our business until afte lunch, and then he proceeded to introduce me to various othe people who were lunching with him. At first I did not thin anything of it. Then suddenly I realised that these men were a connected with the property. One was his solicitor, another h surveyor, a third his accountant and the fourth his agent, thoug not the one I had been dealing with.

It came over me that there was something wrong. I excuse myself and went to the cloakroom. There I re-read a copy of m letter to find out what I had said. I had not specifically mentione in it the number of properties I wanted to buy, and I realise that it might be interpreted to mean something on a larger scal I had to decide whether to ask him to 'spill the beans' there an then or wait until after lunch as he suggested.

I must admit I did not enjoy my lunch much, but from th conversation I did gather that there was a big estate in the back ground. Towards the coffee stage he asked me what I though about it. I said that, before expressing an opinion, there wa certain information I wanted to have. Unfortunately I had com without my plan and particulars; perhaps he could let me have copy? The agent immediately dived under the table, brough out his despatch case and handed me a neatly typed copy of som lengthy particulars and the plan.

I was in a dilemma. Perhaps this was the moment to explair but on the whole I thought that, having gone so far, the best thin was to carry on and hope for the best. I looked at the end of th schedule and found that instead of eight houses there were 860! calculated from the rents that they would have a certain valu and I asked a few obvious questions about road services and s on. Finally I thought I might as well put a bold face on the matte so I asked him how much he wanted for the estate. He said h was rather hoping that I should make an offer, but what he had i mind was between £450,000 and £500,000. I said that from hi conversation at the table I had gathered he had someone else wh vas interested. If so, what was his offer? He replied that he had eceived a bid of £450,000 which he was considering.

Now I thought I saw a way out. I asked him if it was a firm ffer, and after some hesitation he said, 'yes'. I said that in that ase I was afraid I should not be interested as it was far above my rice. He enquired how much I had in mind. From a quick alculation of the rents and particulars, I knew that my price on aper – if I could have bought it – would have been in the region f £400,000. I diffidently mentioned this sum to the owner. He aid he could not consider selling at that figure, and we parted on uite amicable terms, although I noticed that when I got away I vas perspiring.

I have since been careful about accepting luncheon appointnents to discuss business. There was a sequel to this experience. everal years later we were staying at Vilar in Switzerland. I had a ery bad attack of toothache and finally had to hire a taxi to go nto Montreux to see a dentist. As I was leaving the hotel a man ame out and asked if I would mind if he went with me. I said I hould be pleased to have his company. On the way down he aid: 'You know, I've seen you somewhere before.' I said: 'I ravel about a good deal, but I don't remember you.' He replied: I'm an engineer. Does that convey anything to you?' I said: 'No, ut I'm in property.' 'Ah', he said, 'I know! You lunched with me t the Savoy two or three years ago when I tried to sell you an state at Erith.' Then I remembered him. I did not know he was n engineer, but that would explain why he was so unorthdox in is negotiations and why he had his professional men with him. thought I would not say anything about my side of the transacion. I simply said: 'I'm rather curious to know if the bid you had f £450,000 matured?' He said: 'No, I thought it was a firm ffer at the time I told you, but it went off. As a matter of fact you id me a good turn. I used your offer of £400,000 to get another uyer to pay £10,000 more.'

The most important milestone of my career was the year 1926. was not to realise until afterward just how important it was. I ad been approached by a small syndicate, enquiring if I would be nterested in joining them in the purchase of an estate of 137 houses which was at West Hartlepool.

I agreed and went to value the property. The houses were goo but there was, at that time, a slump in shipbuilding and co sequently bad cases of rent arrears. Nevertheless it was agree that if I could possibly get the estate for my assessment figure o £25,000, this would allow a profit margin, possibly of £25 fo each house.

I realised this was a testing of my skill in assessment, and arrived at the auction in some trepidation. The estate was spl into ten lots, and the one I wanted was the first to be auctione I had noticed how few people there were in the room, and luckil the property was knocked down to me for £2,000 less than I wa prepared to give.

When I signed the contract, the auctioneer surprisingly invite me to lunch, which I thought unusual and I wondered if h might have been checking my financial credentials. When I aske him who had bought the other nine lots, he said: 'You did!' I ha not noticed they were to be offered in one lot, but if not taken up only then were they to be offered in separate lots. They were a corner sites for building. I sold them for about £1,000 each an with a mortgage on the residue, it was only necessary to fin £1,000 when completion took place.

From these small beginnings, the Bradford Property Trust Lt was formed in 1928, and in 1981 the assets of the company were i excess of £60m, with a profit for the year of £3½m.

I now decided to close down my estate agency and work ful time as a property dealer. One member of the syndicate of the ne Bradford Property Trust was Algernon Denham. He was the manager of the Bradford branch of the Union Bank of Mancheste and became interested when I opened a £2,000 deposit accoun there. Aware that most people in the estate business at that tim were borrowers, he wanted to have a talk with me to learn m special recipe for successful trading. This was what I had hope for when opening the deposit account.

Mr Denham later told me that when he started his career, he wa earning £1 a week as a bank clerk and when he married he wa only earning £2 a week. A few years later he was manager of th

Bradford branch of the Union Bank of Manchester, and shortly afterwards he was made a director of the Halifax Building Society, of which, years later, he was to become chairman. Eventually he became a director of the main board of Barclays Bank.

With a view to improving my status I had become a freemason and also joined the Liberal Club. I wanted to get to know people of financial standing. It enabled me to further my acquaintance with Mr Denham, who seemed to me the most important up-and-coming man. When I met him it was more than instinct that made me realise here was a man I should cultivate. It was also respect for the way he had climbed the ladder. I was several rungs up at that time and I felt convinced he would help me on my way to the top. Years later this was proved right.

It was due to my first meeting with him that I became involved in the West Hartlepool sale, just reported. At the start, the Bradford Property Trust story is mainly the story of Algy Denham and myself. Although for the first few months after the company was formed he had only a small nominal holding, it was his direction that formed the policy of the company and laid the foundation of its success. It was as a result of his masterminding that the Bradford Trust survived when so many companies, founded at the same time, failed.

The premises of the Union Bank of Manchester were then in what appeared to be a converted shop, but by sheer personality, Algernon Denham, or A.D. as he was known to his close associates, had built up the business to become a rival to other banks. When rumours were circulating that Barclays were negotiating to take over the Union Bank of Manchester, A.D. thought this amalgamation might not suit his future prospects.

The Anglo-South-American Bank had fine premises in Bradford, and was reputed to be in difficulties, so A.D. asked me to go to London to assess the situation. I became friendly with Mr Wells, the managing director, who explained that the bank had started with premises only in London with funds of £6m, and that they had decided to establish a foothold in the Bradford textile trade.

One of his Bradford customers was thought to have borrowed

£1m and then shortly afterwards run into difficulties. This was
time of acute depression in the textile trade and it was the norma
practice for wool merchants to discuss their situation with th
bank manager once a week. It was known as 'going into th
sweating box'. When a friend encountered this particular custome
emerging from the bank he said: 'Hasta bin in t'sweating bo
Billy?' 'Aye', replied Billy. 'I have that lad, but t'other bugger'
sweating.'

Mr Wells had promised to let me know if, and when, th
Bradford premises came on the market and I received a messag
one Saturday morning on a rare occasion when A.D. was away
offering us the premises for £50,000. I knew they had cos
£110,000 to build. I offered £45,000 which was accepted tha
same day.

A.D. was, of course, very pleased with the 'buy' and set abou
using it as a lever to establish his own position. He offered th
premises to Barclays Bank, who flatly turned it down. They alread
had substantial premises nearby which they were about t
reconstruct and did not need another branch in that area. Un
fortunately for them, the outbreak of war in 1939 meant per
mission for reconstruction was withdrawn. They were now gla
to take advantage of our previous offer of the Anglo-South
American bank premises. They paid £47,000 and this include
favourable terms for our own accommodation in the building.

A.D. then became district manager of Barclays Bank and late
chairman of the local board and eventually a full time director o
the bank, where, I understand, he did not ingloriously.

> The heights by great men climbed and kept
> Were not attained by sudden flight.
> But they, while their companions slept
> Were toiling upwards in the night.

Algernon Denham typified the best class of Yorkshireman
Some considered him hard, but he was always just and fair. H
never wasted words. If I put a proposition to him, he woul
listen; then if not interested he would change the subject. I

ressed he might say he would think about it. He had a balanced nind, playing for safety yet with a long-term outlook.

Except for an occasional game of golf, he had very little hysical exercise, but he enjoyed mental exercise. I only knew im to have one week's holiday abroad in thirty years. I have lways taken longer holidays and he claimed that the only time e got a holiday was when I went for one! We met every morning or coffee and he would solve my business problems at the same ime as he solved *The Times* crossword. If I had a difficult letter, e would ring for his secretary and dictate a perfect reply.

It was fatal to try to outwit Mr Denham. A typical instance was ne Saturday morning when he sent for a bright young man on is staff. 'I want you to exercise your fertile mind on this problem nd let me have your answer on Monday morning', he said. When he young man returned on Monday he said: 'Excuse me sir, I vasn't quite sure whether you asked me to exercise my fertile or ny futile mind?' Mr Denham replied: 'I shouldn't worry your ead about that Jones, I probably said one and meant the other.'

There is no doubt he was a financial genius. His method revented the company from overplaying its hand, but at the same ime allowed it to 'bid up to its paper' as bridge players say. Thus, ach estate was financed separately on a repayment basis of nine nonths, when it was usually found possible to sell off sufficient f the property to repay any loan within the time limit.

An instance of his foresight occurred in the early 'thirties, luring the depression. To give a lift to the economy, the Governnent passed a bill known as the 1933 Act. This was to encourage uilders to erect small houses to let at low rentals. The Governnent would guarantee a 100 per cent mortgage at 5 per cent, epayable over a thirty-year term, but the rents had to be no nore than 10s a week. This offer was turned down by builders, uilding societies and investors, who considered the terms nerous and the profits negligible.

Whilst it was considered two risky for the Bradford Property Trust, Mr Denham thought there might be something in it over a ong term. Four of us invested £500 each, then left everything in A.D.'s hands.

He bought a site for forty-four houses and then got out plan
and specifications for two types, some semi-detached, whic
would be let at 10s a week, and some in terraces of six whic
would be let at 7s 6d a week. Mr Denham supervised all th
specifications down to the last door knob and the cost of eac
house averaged £275. Then he took over the estate and the non
executive investors came out with a small profit.

Up until then the Bradford Property Trust had not considere
building houses, but with these specifications in front of us, w
knew we could build houses to sell at prices ranging approxi
mately from £375 to £475. In consequence, we were responsibl
for building hundreds of houses in various parts of the country.

> Great vessels may venture more
> But little boats must keep near shore.

Algernon Denham was not only the mainspring of the Bradfor
Property Trust, but so far as finance was concerned, he was th
whole team plus the dog under the wagon. The basis of th
company was economy. He took no salary for ten years and I, a
managing director, received £1,000pa. He had a frugal streak in hi
make-up. On his visits to London he would send to the bank fo
£1 of sixpences for tips, but he rarely used more than five of them
We both stayed at the Dean Hotel, Oxford Street at a cost o
7s 6d a night, including a full English breakfast.

The London office was a converted terrace house in Waltham
stow, while the boardroom in Bradford is still used as a secretary'
office today.

By way of bonus, the rent collectors were given £1 commissio
on the sale of a house to a tenant. This meant spending night
trying to persuade tenants to buy for, say, £300, a house whicl
would be worth £10,000 a year or two later.

Subsequently shares in the company were substituted fo
commission, and, of course, they eventually turned out to be ver
valuable.

In 1928 I was fortunate to be elected a director of what wa
then the Bradford Second Equitable Building Society (nov

nown as the Bradford and Bingley Building Society).

I was then the youngest member of the board by thirty years. he assets of the Society at that time were about £4m. I retired om this board at the age of eighty. Today the assets of the ociety are well over a billion.

Not only has this long association with the building-society ovement been important to me in my business career; it has also ought me many valued friendships and I can look back on the appy times spent with people I have met.

The new company was now firmly established and, quite by ance, we found an opportunity of doing business on a much rger scale. Many of the large industrial concerns owned estates houses which had been built so that employees could live near eir work. A large proportion of these tenants were now unem-oyed or had taken other jobs. The houses were let at very low nts and the tenants were protected by the Rent Act. Not only d such property produce an uneconomic return; it was a drain n a firm's resources at a difficult time. We were now entering e slump period of the 'thirties; unemployment was rife and en the best firms had difficulty in surviving.

Mr Denham came into contact with the textile firm of Saltaire, wning 1,000 houses of this sort. In reconstructing their business ey were trying to find some way to dispose of their property, d at the same time to protect their employees and pensioners. saw the managing director and suggested we should buy the tate. We would guarantee not to disturb any tenants to whom ey had an obligation, and in addition everyone would have the portunity of purchasing at a margin over cost of £25 a house. he idea appealed to the company and eventually we bought on ose terms. During the negotiations there was a £10,000 fference between our price and theirs, but when I pointed out at it would be the tenants who would suffer, as the price of the ouse would be £10 more, the owners accepted our price.

This estate presented new problems. It was sixty years old d had once been a model village, but by this time it badly eeded modernising. Sanitary facilities and services wanted newing and the backs of the houses were enclosed with high

stone walls which had to be lowered to let in more light. Alt-
gether we had to spend £100,000 before the estate could l
offered for resale. For this expenditure we received very litt
extra income because of the Rent Act, though a large majority
the tenants bought their houses from us. This was a valuab
experience and there is no doubt that our work extended the li
of the property by at least half a century.

I have no wish to weary readers with long accounts of proper
deals – the basic pattern, once formed, reasserted itself again ar
again. We bought large numbers of houses from textile firm
steel companies, railway concerns, and in fact I know of no lar
estate owned by an industrial company which has not been sold
us if it came on to the market after this. We have specialised
renovating and modernising this class of property ever since. I
addition we acquired several large estates in London and th
provinces which had been built as offshoots of the Hampste
Garden Suburb. These properties were modernised and dealt wi
in the same way. Altogether, we have sold some 25,000 to 30,0
houses to tenants, and none of them to my knowledge has lost
penny on the resale; in fact, many of them realised twice ar
three times the purchase price originally paid.

We also financed the building of many hundreds of small hous
for industrial concerns before the Second World War, on the o
principle of £25 per house margin. For example, our price for
new house with two bedrooms, a sitting-room, kitchen, sculler
bathroom and so on was from £365 to £400.

It is said appetite grows on what it feeds, and we were no
tempted to extend our activity to dealing with other types
property. I experimented with buying freehold ground rents ar
on one occasion paid £6,000 for an income of a penny a year. Th
of course had valuable reversion in five years.

Whilst Mr Denham was a big believer in 'every man to his last
he was not against trying a new venture, and one of these tran
actions gave us an insight into the hotel industry. This was th
lease of Mount Royal, a block of 650 luxury flats at the back
Oxford Street next to the Cumberland Hotel. These were fo
short-stay accommodation; each flat had a bed-sitting room

athroom and kitchen. A restaurant, a grocery and other shops
ere included in the block.

The flats were to be let on a weekly basis. A hotelier had taken
lease of the premises and needed capital, so my colleagues and I
rmed a company to raise the capital. I had a supervisory
irectorship, whilst the hotelier was appointed managing director.
ne of the first jobs was to buy the furniture, for which A.D. was
ainly responsible. It was during the depths of the depression and
consequence we were able to acquire high-class furniture at a
w price. A firm, now well known, but then just starting up in
usiness, allowed us to have 1,000 beds at £5 15s each, provided
e allowed them to use in their advertisement: 'As supplied
Mount Royal'.

When we opened we were fully booked at £3 3s per flat per
eek, and we kept a few to let at 12s 6d a night including break-
st. I had no previous experience of running a place of this size
nd, whilst I was not responsible for the actual management, I
ad to keep an eye on the financial side. We did very well the first
ear, but we found one or two weaknesses in the organisation
hich we could not put right.

One was the uncertainty of the restaurant trade. Some days it
ould be full; other days everybody would decide either to have
eir meals in their flats or to go elsewhere. The other snag was
orse. We found that the rent was too close a fit with the over-
eads. We had to be over 90 per cent full all the year round,
hereas an ordinary hotel could perhaps pay its way with a
apacity of 60 per cent. We had only four slack weeks in the year,
wo in August, and two at Christmas, but during those weeks our
akings dropped by more than £4,000.

I envy no one the money they make in the hotel industry. It is
ndeed a highly specialised business. We sold the lease without
egrets in 1938.

We also began experimenting in agricultural estates. One of our
arliest deals was a large one of 18,000 acres, including Rufford
Abbey, a valuable property with colliery rights and a large area of
imber. There were four villages, four advowsons, the famous
Hop Pole Hotel, and several public houses. It was a lock-stock-

and-barrel purchase, embracing rare furniture, pictures, a
extensive library and what appeared to be very fine cellar
Unfortunately the wine had not been kept in the right conditio
and much of it had become ullaged.

This gave me an exciting insight into a world of which I kne
virtually nothing – the art business. After the purchase I learne
something about antiques that might have stopped us fro
buying. We assumed that, when the contents of the mansio
had been scheduled and valued for probate by an eminent firm
valuers, we could reasonably expect to realise something ne
that figure.

Knight, Frank & Rutley were the auctioneers and I w
disconcerted to be told that the market value might not represe
anything like the probate value. Paintings, *objets d'art* and oth
antiques did not attract death duties, so that these items we
valued high to suit the whim of the owners. The estate had been i
the same family since before the fourteenth century, and while w
had pictures signed by well-known artists, it was not certain ho
many of them were genuine. Pictures reproduced in the catalog
were genuine. Pictures of doubtful origin had a reserve price
£100. It turned out that some of the latter were genuine, but ha
been painted over. The auctioneer told me there was always or
pleasant surprise of this kind in a sale, and so it turned out this tim

First we had a five-day sale at the Abbey, to dispose of th
chattels and less valuable furnishings. In spite of the threat
war, it was attended by all the leading dealers, and satisfacto
prices were realised. Even so, we recovered only a quarter
what we paid for the furniture and everything else depended o
the separate sale at Christie's of the pictures, tapestries and othe
objets d'art. Unfortunately all these due for sale were destroyed b
a bomb.

One lady at the sale was buying most of the furniture an
tapestries for a large hall she was about to occupy in the distric
Her method of purchasing began by ringing the porter to th
auction and instructing him to bid to a certain price. Afterward
her secretary would arrive and decide whether to go furthe
Finally, if she thought fit, she would come herself and pay ye

ıore. In one instance they overbid each other by £300 which we eturned.

Items were put up for sale every day, china one day, pictures the ext, and the contents of the bedrooms were split up. This special urchaser had been buying everything from the bedroom which ad always been reserved for King Edward VII on his many visits) Rufford Abbey. Items in this bedroom were either of gold or old-coloured and included among the furniture was a four-poster ed. The day she rang up to make her bids, the porter reminded er that the bed was to be put up for sale, but she said she wasn't ıterested. We had put on a reserve of £60, but as we had no ther prospective buyer it was knocked down to me. There was ne genuine offer of £50, so I approached this bidder to ask if e was interested enough to offer £60. His wife was anxious) have the bed as she had a sentimental attachment to the Abbey. Ie said he would think it over and let me know after lunch.

Immediately he had gone, a friend of our expected customer ıshed in. 'Has the bed gone?' she asked. It seems that our ıstomer's car had broken down on her way to the sale, so she ad telephoned this friend asking her to bid up to £100 for the ed. I explained the situation and when the man returned from ınch he had decided to buy the bed. I told him I could get a rofit of £10 if he would part with it, but he was not interested. then offered £100 for the bed, but he was adamant in his refusal) sell.

Three days later when he was loading up his purchases in a antechnicon, I said: 'What about the bed?' He replied: 'Oh, I t the old lady have it. She pestered me night and day.' When I sked: 'How much did she pay?' He gave a sly smile. '£300', e said.

The mansion itself was up for auction as a separate lot. This ıcluded timber valued at £18,000, 800 acres of parkland and ıirteen service cottages with up-to-date facilities. As we wanted) achieve a sale, we were prepared to accept the low figure f £32,000.

The night before the auction, I was staying at a nearby hotel ith the auctioneer, when we were approached by a speculator

who, after some negotiation, offered £30,000. In the normal wa
it is not considered a sale until the contract is signed and a depos
paid, but I knew the speculator and decided to run the risk.

He arranged for his son-in-law, who was a solicitor, to com
the next morning, when he would sign the contract and pay th
deposit.

On arriving, the son-in-law queried a small item relating to th
electricity supply. I got in touch with the Electricity Board an
the matter was settled satisfactorily.

By this time I had cancelled the auction, but the prospectiv
buyer and his son-in-law had disappeared. We continued to wai
but in vain. The next morning I received this note.

Re: *Rufford Abbey Estate*

Not proceeding.

The mansion was subsequently sold to an investor, wh
rented it to the War Office during the war. The parkland wa
ploughed up and selected portions of the timber sold.

Fortunately, there had been other assets on the estate whic
increased in value during the war and eventually we came ou
with a small profit on the venture.

The Eagle Star Insurance Company lent us £300,000 toward
the purchase of Rufford Abbey Estate, at the normal rate c
5 per cent plus a share of the profits, but at the end of the nin
month's settlement date, we had to pay very little as a larg
amount of the residue remained unsold.

On a previous occasion the Eagle Star had loaned us £100,00
at 5 per cent interest. This money was useful to us, but when th
bank rate fell, A.D., who believed in 'money saved is mone
earned', suggested I should see the chairman, Sir Edwar
Mountain, and ask him to reduce our rate to 4 per cent.

Sir Edward, who was cast in the same mould as A.D., said
'How long notice did I give you for repayment of this loan?'
said: 'I thought it was a month.' He replied: 'Take the notic
from now.' A.D. was not unduly perturbed by this and when Si
Edward asked to see me again three weeks later, A.D. said: '

:now what he wants, settle for 4½ per cent.' This I did.

Sir Edward had benefited, however, from the Rufford Abbey ale, where he purchased a picture for £450 which recently sold t Christie's for £288,000.

After the outbreak of war, buying and selling property was lmost at a standstill, but there was a certain amount of activity n agricultural estates. I was, by this time, farming myself in a mall way and I found that, with my hereditary background, I had n instinct for assessing land values. For instance, I had a good dea just by walking over land whether its pre-war rental value vas 5s an acre or £2 an acre. Also I could calculate the acreage of any field up to 40 acres at a glance by visualising our own -acre field and mentally multiplying or dividing it. I had also pent a week scaring crows on a 40-acre. Today, I want nothing etter in assessing the value of an estate than to walk over it with farm labourer who has worked on it for a number of years.

During the war we bought several large agricultural estates in lifferent parts of the country and, after the end of hostilities, this ection started to expand rapidly, which meant enlarging our rganisation. Two separate land companies were formed, and we vere fortunate in acquiring as managing director a young man vith a first-rate academic knowledge, combined with a wide xperience of this specialised business.

This also gave an opportunity for my son Peter, and A.D's 'ounger son, Eric Denham, to enter the business on their return rom war service, and they are now directors of the parent ompanies.

Over the years I have found buying in an auction can be xciting and nerve racking. Some years ago I attended the auction of a large agricultural estate which attracted many of the important uyers in the country. It was for sale as a whole or in lots, and in onsequence all the tenants turned up with their families to try to uy their holdings if the estate was not sold in one lot.

The town hall, where the sale was to take place, was packed. 'here must have been more than 500 people there, including an rray of the leading members of the estate agents' profession. 'here were also many surveyors and solicitors who were busy

with their clients, examining plans and maps. It seemed impossibl
that an insignificant person like myself should attempt to compet
with this galaxy of brains and wealth. The auctioneer and hi
retinue of advisers, solicitors, agents and clerks made a very impos
ing spectacle on the rostrum. Although I have been to score
of auctions I still feel nervous tension before the sale begins.

The opening bid in this case was £100,000. Dealers do not tak
much notice of the proceedings in the early stages, although th
auctioneer is very alert in trying to size up the field and sor
out the genuine buyers. The auction proceeded by gradual stage
up to £150,000. I then sat up and began to take notice. It wa
obvious that genuine bids were coming in. When they reache
£160,000 there came the magic announcement that the propert
was in the market and would be sold, which meant that there wa
a genuine bid and the reserve had been reached.

My limit was £175,000, so I had £15,000 in hand and I wante
to give away as little as possible. I looked round to try and fin
out how many bidders were involved. I recognised three or fou
still making the running. The bids were coming in at £1,000
time. At this stage I put in a bid to let the auctioneer know I wa
there, and then sat back and watched until the amount reache
£170,000. By this time, the field had narrowed down to mysel
and two others. Unfortunately, when my limit of £175,000 wa
reached there was still one competitor who was bidding wit
confidence. I knew him well as one of the astutest land valuers i
England. I thought he must be nearing his limit and I woul
risk another £1,000 or two. My price was based to allow me
10 per cent profit for resale piecemeal and what is known a
'adventurer's risk'. This margin does not allow for much discoun
and every £1,000 bid from now on meant so much less profit, bu
I knew that I was following a good buyer and could not be fa
wrong. In a small deal he might have run me up and left me wit
it, but this was too big for him to take the risk. I thought I woul
risk up to 5 per cent of my profit, which meant that I could go t
£182,000, but when I reached this figure he was still biddin
confidently. I had to think quickly. I realised that there wa
something wrong and that I must have missed something.

lanced at the income schedule and decided that he could not ossibly be relying only on the rent roll. A hoarse voice in my ar whispered: 'She'll split up for 200.' This came from the local gent who had been advising me. I saw his point; the tenants vere obviously interested and might pay more. I dropped my ext bid from £1,000 to £500 to give me a chance to think. There nust be some extra value somewhere – and I decided it was imber. There was a large area of woodland and we had not had a hance to get a proper valuation. By this time, the bidding was 188,000, and I thought I must stop now. I realised that my pponent's limit must be £190,000. The auctioneer lifted his ammer for the third time, looked at me, as did every eye in the oom and said: 'The bidding is against you at £188,000.' The nly excuse I could find for going further was that if it was worth to my competitor it must be to me. I said to myself: 'It is muck r the golden crown.' I bid £190,000. My opponent for the first ime was shaken. His confidence had gone. He hesitated. Again he hammer was on the way down – when he said '192'.

I sat back with a relieved sigh. This time I had definitely nished, and I was certain there could be nothing left in it for nyone. My opponent came up to me immediately afterwards and aid, 'Were you bidding for yourself?' and I told him that I was. Then he asked: 'How on earth could you go to that figure? I have one £2,000 over my limit.'

I did not say how much I had gone over mine, but asked: 'What ave you got up your sleeve anyway?'

He replied: 'It isn't up my sleeve, it's in my pocket. I had made rrangements with the tenants to pay an increase of rent if I ought.'

In the train going to London I travelled with several of the eading estate agents. They congratulated me on a narrow shave, nd said I was a very lucky man. One of my agent friends said: We are going to celebrate your escape when we get to town. I am oing to treat you to a champagne dinner.' We went to Romano's nd had our bottle of champagne. On the other side of the room vere our erstwhile opponent and his friends. They were having a nagnum. When I spoke to him later he said he was quite satisfied with his deal. He asked me: 'What was your valuation of th timber?' '£40,000', I replied, 'We had it measured and it came ou at £60,000', he then told me. The estate turned out even bette than his optimistic valuation.

Dealing in landed estates is a fascinating and hazardous business The speculator takes his profit or his medicine. As a successfu Yorkshire dealer said on being reminded of a loss: 'He's a foo when he doesn't know when it's ower.'

The important thing is to buy right. Poor land cannot b bought cheap enough. I have sold land at £2 an acre which cos more than £50 an acre to make it productive. It was then wortl less than land which could have been bought at £30 an acre. O the other hand fertile loam and silt land is worth more today tha at any time and often produces twice the yield for the same see and labour, with a consequently higher profit margin.

Buying and selling land and properties necessitates spendin much time in the auction room. There is nothing more exhilaratin than a successful auction and nothing more depressing than a abortive one. In offering agricultural estates much depends on th tenants' reactions. Experience has taught me not to disarrang tenants' holdings when splitting up for resale. They objec strongly to this 'interference with nature'. One mistake I made i this respect was just before the war when dealing with a larg estate of poorish land. It was a three-day sale and we were into th second day before we received an acceptable offer for any lot.

Most of the land had been open fields in the old days. Thes had been split up and let off to different tenants. As a result ther had been considerable overlapping and each of the farms ha many scattered fields. These are known as four-day farms becaus it takes the workers two days every week to get to and from thei work. We thought it would be a good opportunity whilst it wa in one ownership to block the land so that each farm would hav the same acreage in a self-contained unit. This would provid easy access and be more economical to work. This was done an although the price was only £10 an acre, none of the tenant would buy because they did not agree with the way the lan offered to them was lotted. For instance, they all complained tha hey had not got their proper share of grassland. Also that the land hey were expected to take over from their neighbours had been adly farmed. It was several years before we eventually got ut. By good fortune it was the only area in England where oil vas found in commercial quantities and whilst striking oil in this ountry brings no benefit to the owner, the land was taken over y the oil company concerned for refinery and storage purposes.

An auctioneer can usually sense from the atmosphere after the irst few minutes whether the auction is going to be successful. Oral bids, even if they are low, are always a good sign. The display f finesse on the part of the auctioneer and his audience is always nteresting. To create confidence he usually starts by suggesting price of much more than the property's real worth. Supposing e says: 'Who will give me an opening bid of £10,000?' The rospective buyer does some swift mental calculations. He says to imself: 'He is asking 10, he means 8, he will take 6, it's worth 4, 'll offer him 2.' Although the auctioneer may appear to be hocked by this low figure, he accepts the bid and then tries to ind another man who wants a bargain. If he does not succeed, he robably makes one or two bogus bids until he gets somewhere ear the reserve, when he turns to the original bidder and com-romises at around £5,000.

Auctions without reserve are rarely announced these days, but n war time it was quite a common occurrence in areas where there vas special risk to property.

Although I have been over fifty years in and out of auction ooms, both buying and selling property, I have only been nvolved on three occasions in sales without reserve. The first ne, I was buying, the other two, selling. I bought what today vould be regarded as a good bargain, but it turned out that it flattered to deceive'. In the second, I lost money, and in the third ase, on paper I made far too much.

It was quite by chance I became the owner of Roxholm Hall nd estate for £1,000. I had noticed in the paper that this small state, near to my native village, was up for sale, and out of uriosity I wrote for particulars. The agent who sent the catalogue, vhich described the Hall as in good condition, with 70 acres and two good cottages, told me he thought it would go cheap. I replied that I had merely sent for the catalogue out of curiosity and was not interested in buying.

About a week before the auction was due to take place, he rang me up and asked me if I would make an offer. The owners were hoping to get £10,000 but might take less. Instead of employing the auctioneer's special arithmetic mentioned previously and offering him £2,000, as I didn't want the property I halved this figure and made him an offer of £1,000. The agent thought this ridiculous, so I replied: 'Well it will start you off'. However, it appeared that no one turned up at the auction, and therefore I became the owner.

It was some time before I was to inspect the Hall. I looked up some historical sources, and found there was a record of the Hall dated 1825; it then appeared to be about 500 years old. I read that the mansion retained all the character of former times and had many charms for the antiquary, having been built on the site of an old monastery.

Eventually, when I happened to be in the district, I called to inspect the property and was agreeably surprised to find two excellent cottages and that the carriage drive was well made and kept in condition. I was more than surprised, on approaching the Hall, to find that it was not only occupied, but that there was a garden party in progress. It was a summer's day and tennis was being played, the guests having tea on the lawn. I thought surely I must have made a mistake.

I made my way to the front and found the hostess, and said I was sorry to intrude, but was this the place I had bought? On hearing my name she said 'Oh, yes, we have been waiting for you, but we thought we would like to keep everything in order until you came to occupy it.' She was rather sad when I told her I had no intention of doing so; she obviously had a good deal of sentimental affection for the place. It was only when I wanted to sell it that I found the snag. It was almost on top of Cranwell aerodrome and, with war in prospect, not even the personnel of the airfield cared to occupy it. I eventually sold it to a lady who bred dogs.

My first sale without reserve was the contents of a well-furnished ottage in my native village. Having sold the cottage, I told the uctioneer he could sell the contents without reserve. In due ourse I received a cheque for £15 for the total sale price. Fornately it was not of any consequence to me, but I was curious to now what had happened. It appeared it was not sufficiently dvertised outside the village, and the inhabitants had decided to plit it up among themselves, and I found that the highest price aid for any one item was £2 for a suite of furniture.

The other sale was very much more important, and had repercussions for many years. It was the residue of two large estates – hat is, what speculators call 'odds and sods'. We had already eceived a moiety from these estates – that is, the adventurer's rofit of 10 per cent – and I thought I would take a risk, and at the ame time have some fun in selling the remainder without reserve.

It was a miscellaneous collection comprising a small-holding, abourers' cottages, a few ground rents, small woodlands, a uarry, and even an advowson. The most important thing about sale without reserve is that the would-be buyers are convinced hat the sale is genuine. In this case everybody in the area knew hat the auctioneer was a man of integrity, and would only ccept genuine bids. We expected to raise about £10,000. The rst lot was put up and received a bid of £100, and when the uctioneer asked for more offers a voice said £199 10s. The lot vas knocked down to this bidder. I assumed this man to be a peculator because they have a habit, if they particularly want nything, of confusing the ordinary bidder by jumping to a much igher figure. The next lot was put up and £200 was bid, and hen this same voice said £350, and again the lot was knocked own to him. The third lot was the quarry, for which I knew here was a genuine buyer, a local man wanting the stone for naking a road in the vicinity. We had a first bid of £450 which ve assumed came from the genuine buyer, and it was just about o be knocked down when the voice called £950 and again the lot vas knocked down to him. I then had a brief consultation with the uctioneer and said wasn't something very much wrong – people vere not getting a chance to buy. Was this man genuine? The

auctioneer said he knew him quite well; he had attended many o
his auctions and had been a very good buyer. We decided that th
only thing to do was to try to ignore him where possible. Afte
that we did get quite a few outside people buying, and the tota
at the end of the sale was £15,000, against the expected amount o
£10,000, but when reckoned up, £10,000 of this had been sol
to our freak buyer. He paid his 10 per cent deposit to the auction
eer of £1,000, but the next day we heard he had gone into a menta
home and in due course his cheque was returned marked 'Refer t
drawer'. This left me in an impossible position. I got in touc
with the man who wanted the quarry, saying we would be pre
pared to accept £500, but he had by then got the required ston
elsewhere. It was twenty years before the left-overs were finall
cleared up.

One transaction which gave me a great deal of satisfaction wa
non-profitable, but stimulating and amusing.

I was a member of Bradford Civic Society when St George'
Hall came up for sale; it was a building of considerable historica
interest and would be an acquisition of importance to the Society
It had been offered to the city council for £100,000 and, althoug
the price was reasonable, they were unable to negotiate becaus
of shortage of money. It was owned by the Rank Organisation
who had been using it as a cinema, which they were now closin
down, and they were having difficulty in selling it.

I was asked to make a valuation with a view to raising th
money privately and then to approach Mr Rank with the offer
The day before my appointment with him, the president of th
Civic Society, Mr Robert Cook, rang up to say they had got cold
feet as the Civic Society could not find enough sponsors to risk
buying it. When I told A.D. that my valuation was £35,000, h
agreed it would be worth buying at that figure whether th
council would take it over or not.

On the morning of my appointment with Mr Rank, he sent an
apology to say he would be a quarter of an hour late. When he
arrived, he told me he had been having lunch with the Chancello
of the Exchequer. I told him I had lunched with Sir Edward
Mountain, who said he was a friend of his. Mr Rank asked: 'Do

ɔu do business with him?' I replied: 'Yes, in the normal way, ut this morning I mentioned I was about to visit you and would e tell me what your weaknesses were.' Sir Edward had said, Ie hasn't any,' which amused Mr Rank.

He began by saying: 'I understand your offer for this property £35,000. You are a surveyor, what would it cost to build today?' said: 'Probably £300,000.' Mr Rank said: 'Surely in that case, it worth £100,000?' I pointed out that in my experience a building as only worth what it could be used for, and as a road planning heme threatened to cut the building in half, it could only be used a warehouse. Mr Rank said he had his shareholders to consider.

'Wouldn't it be better to sell at this price than to hold a deterior-ing asset?' I asked. After further discussion he said he would let e know in a fortnight.

Two weeks later I received a letter stating that the offer was ccepted. I was then able to tell the Civic Society Committee that ey could offer St George's Hall to the council for the exact sum e paid for it. The council very wisely purchased it and, later, the lans for a road to go through the Hall were withdrawn.

Although a great deal of money was subsequently spent on odernising the structure, it was, without doubt, one of the best uys' a corporation ever made.

17
EASING OFF

> Be wise in time, and turn your horse out to grass when h
> shows signs of age, lest he end in a ludicrous breakdown wit
> straining flanks.
>
> HORAC

In the middle of the 1930s I persuaded my colleagues, against the
wishes, to convert our property business into a public compan

We approached one of the best issuing houses and, after
thorough investigation, terms were agreed for the issue o
ordinary and preference shares. The negotiations took longer tha
I expected. I had booked to go to South Africa with my wife, an
when we sailed there was a very small matter which remained u
settled. The head of the issuing house told me that, before I ha
been on the ship two days, I should receive a radio messag
confirming that it was arranged.

That message did not arrive. The day after we left there ha
been a debate in Parliament on Germany, and £200m had bee
voted for armaments. What is a mere flea-bite today in nation
spending was sufficient in the 1930s to cause a deep depression o
the Stock Exchange. It was then decided to wait until my retur
before proceeding further. When I got back to England, aft
discussion among my colleagues and the principals of the issuin
house, we agreed not to proceed with the flotation. It was at th
time that two of the original, non-active shareholders in th
business agreed to be paid out.

If the public issue had materialised I should have been selling
substantial part of my interest in the company, and it had been m
intention in that case to devote part of my time to public worl
Now, instead of reducing my commitments, I found myself mor
heavily involved than ever.

It had nevertheless been on my conscience for some time past at I ought to try to contribute something to the general good. nce or twice I had been invited to seek election to the Bradford uncil and to take part in other public affairs, but as I was away om Bradford a good deal, I had a reasonable excuse for turning ese invitations down. I was well aware of my limitations. For stance, I had little experience of public speaking. It was always a g strain for me, and something for which I never felt I had a tural bent. This is one of the many accomplishments that ould be acquired early in life. I have noticed that people nnected with religious groups, and chapel members in particular, t accustomed early to standing on their feet and so find a tural way of expressing themselves.

I came to the conclusion that I could best serve the community choosing a field within the compass of my knowledge and perience. The one thing I did know something about was operty, so a year or two later, when the Second World War ought me unexpected leisure, I worked on a scheme which I d very much at heart – the redevelopment of slum areas.

I had noticed that in every large town or city, including London, ere were belts of property ringing the centres that had deterior-ed into slums through age and changes in fashion. At the same ne, this property occupied valuable sites. In the new legislation hich had been drafted for rebuilding blitzed property, provision as also made for acquiring and rebuilding all slum areas. eviously, under private enterprise, this could have been carried it only piecemeal.

I therefore worked out a sample scheme for the development of area of 22 acres in Bradford. I spent a lot of time and money on e project, and it took me the best part of a year. I made over 000 valuations of property and paid another surveyor to check y valuations independently. There was only about £50,000 fference between us in a total of nearly £1 million.

The scheme was eventually published in *The Yorkshire Observer* d was printed in pamphlet form. The city council gave it their nsideration. It was suggested that I might recommend someone ho could carry out the scheme, so I got in touch with an archi-

tect who was an enthusiastic town planner. He came to Bradfo:
and addressed the council, but instead of concentrating on tl
particular scheme in hand, he wanted to make it part of a r
planning scheme for the whole of the city, and eventually tl
matter petered out. Perhaps this was my biggest failure. There
no doubt that, had I been big enough to carry the scheme throug
myself, the council would have been only too willing to give me
reasonably free hand. Nor did I find the right man to carry out n
ideas for me.

At the same time I got more satisfaction from working on tl
scheme than anything else I have done outside my own busines
Perhaps, too, the seed sown may have had its effect, for I ha
correspondence about the plan with many other town council
some as far away as Australia.

During the war the property market was at a standstill, and
bought a small farm. I suddenly had a longing to get back to tl
land and to the real things of life. Again, Thoreau's *Walden* was
great standby. I found at first that I could not work for lor
stretches, though I could feel that I was handling the too
naturally. Gradually everything came back to me. I set and picke
potatoes, spread muck, ploughed and harrowed. It was main
a dairy farm, but I had to put part of the land down to the ploug
for corn. To gather the few acres of wheat was a sheer joy for m
and the pleasantest time of all was the haymaking. To my surpri
I found I could work a full day making hay, and although I wa
tired in every limb by night, a refreshing sleep restored me for tl
next spell.

However, it was at Simon's Seat Farm, which I bought a litt
later, that we snatched most of our peaceful, happy days durin
the war. It was near a village with a most intriguing name
Appletreewick. It was overlooked by Simon's Seat, a hill of
few hundred feet high on which, according to the legend,
shepherd had found a child. This child was brought up by tl
villagers and chistened 'Amangam' – the dialect form of 'amon
them'. We even had electricity and central heating and, aft

receiving several airmen who had parachuted down, we we
given a telephone. I shall not forget an airman stumbling out c

e moorland mist into the cottage one January morning, and how lieved he was to find he was in England. He had no idea where : was when he was told to jump.

The only time we were rushed at Simon's Seat was during ymaking. Any man, woman or child in the district would drop for an hour's turning. The foreman's wife was busy all day oviding what was known as 'drinking'. Her tea and sandwiches me up about once an hour. Only people who worked at least ur hours a day were invited to lunch. We had one scrounger ho usually managed to put in the time without doing much ork. On one occasion he invited himself to lunch with the reman and our neighbours. They had roly-poly pudding that y, and the foreman said to the scrounger: 'Dost a like ends?' o which he replied, 'No'. 'Well', said the foreman, 'me and my l does', and he divided the pudding into two halves.

It was from Simon's Seat that we set out on a memorable and ten comic pony-and-trap tour.

At that time, of course, there was no petrol for pleasure trips, so went to an auction and bought an elegant governess car and its ddlery, but to my consternation the pony that went with them, high stepper, fetched £150, which was too steep for me. However I knew the auctioneer and told him afterwards of my iandary. He said he thought he could fix me up. I said I wanted mething that would go with the trap, but not necessarily a iowpiece.

A little later a skewbald pony arrived. He really looked the part, I left it to my foreman to take him for a trial run. He reported at he did not think there was anything radically wrong with the ony, but that he was afraid he was 'no journeyman'. I said that is did not disturb me unduly. We were going to do only about venty-five miles a day. Although I had never been long distances yself in a pony and trap, some friends of mine talked of jog-otting to Morecambe, sixty miles away, in a day.

We arranged to take with us a bag of oats and a large bag of iaff in case they were not available where we stabled for the ight, and of course we took a nosebag for outdoor feeding. We ad a lot of luggage of our own.

I bought a long slender whip. This was intended for orname
only, as I knew that with well-bred horses it was consider
rather unseemly to use the whip except in a playful way to fli
the ears or give a gay crack when bowling through a village. T
usual practice is to talk to the horse in its own language, with
occasional rustle of the reins or, at the worst, a shaking of t
whip-socket. You would never think of actually striking a we
bred horse. You might get violent reactions.

Just as we were about to start, we realised that we had omitt
to get to know the pony's name, so we had to look up the bill
purchase. It was described as 'an upstanding well-bred Dal
skewbald of thirteen hands', but it had no other identificatio
This meant we should start off as strangers. Ponies are ve
sensitive to a name of their own. It makes them one of the famil
and if you know the name, even if you are not intimate, at lea
it puts you in the position of being a friend of a friend of theirs.

Unquestionably we were quite a smart turn-out as we trotte
off from Appletreewick. It was a beautiful spring morning; bir
were singing, and all the world was young. Farmers and the
wives and children came out of their houses to greet us as w
passed or waved to us from the fields. Everything seemed to
set for a happy and carefree holiday.

Our first stop was to be Giggleswick, about twenty-five mil
away. I purposely arranged these short distances so that we shou
not be tempted to overwork the pony. I knew that I could sa
about five miles by taking a short cut over the moors. This w
rather a rough road with some steep inclines, but I had been ov
it by car and felt there was no real obstacle. When we got to th
track a minor problem presented itself; we found that the balan
did not work out right on the hills. There was too much weig
at the back, and this had the effect of lifting the pony slightly o
the road going up-hill and of pressing him down into it as w
descended. My wife was concerned about this, but I assured h
it was just one of the things ponies were used to.

We had gone about two miles on this rough road when, halfwa
up a steep hill, we suddenly came to a dead stop for no appare
reason. I explained to my wife that horses very often stopp

n personal impulses, or perhaps just for a breather. However, :ter waiting some time, I started urging the pony forward – ·ithout the slightest effect. The large bag of chaff in front of the ·ap prevented us from seeing anything but the pony's ears as we ·ere going uphill. I suggested to my wife that she should take the :ins while I went to investigate. This she declined to do saying: f you are going to abandon the trap, then I am getting out too.'

Strangely enough, the moment we both got out the pony 1oved swiftly forward. My wife pointed out the mark of the body elt and suggested that the poor beast had not been able to get its reath. When we got to the top of the hill we decided that we 1ust throw something overboard.

After due consideration we discarded the bag of chaff. We 1ought we could not afford to be short of oats, but that we could robably get chaff. This was a mistake. In all our travels nobody ad any chaff, but everybody had oats.

We had learnt our lesson about hills, and afterwards we either ery quickly transferred large pieces of luggage from the back to he front when we came to a hill, or got out and walked.

In spite of all the care and attention we were lavishing on the ·ony, it seemed to be getting more and more depressed and ·ilting badly. To give it a rest we decided to have lunch earlier han we had intended, so we out-spanned at twelve o'clock. The ·ony brightened up considerably when he saw the nosebag. He ·as obviously touched by this thoughtfulness, and we hoped that, :nowing us better, he would collaborate a little more cordially n the afternoon.

We were now set for the last lap of the day, about twelve niles. The pony did very well for the first two or three and then ell away again badly, so that by now, instead of sitting back and njoying the scenery, I was spending all my time talking to him, ·ulling the reins and rattling the whip-socket.

I even thought of using the whip but did not want to do this :xcept as a last resort; it would leave me without anything in eserve. In the end I had to start gingerly flicking the whip, but t made little difference. Eventually I gave the pony a very lefinite hit. The result surprised me. It made not the slightest

difference, and I began to wonder if the pony was as highly-bre
as I had been led to believe.

There was only one way to get him over the last five mile
This was not to lead him but to drag him, for by this time he w
not only drooping at the head and shoulders, but also saggin
at the knees.

It was a great relief when we arrived at the hotel. After dinn
and a bottle of wine we felt better. My wife said that she did n
think I knew quite as much about ponies as I had implied. I sai
he reminded me of the Irish fire brigade horse who:

> . . . . had a funny gait with him, an action all his own,
> It was something between walking very slow and leaving it alon
> This is how he went on level ground; when he had to climb,
> We had to get out and help the creeter every time.
> We used to tie him up behind when going down a hill,
> For fear we overtook him. He was best at standing still.

After much tribulation we arrived the next evening at
celebrated old coaching-house in Kirkby Lonsdale. It was dar
when we got in, and we left the pony in the stable and tried t
forget about it until morning. While we were having dinne
however, the waiter came along and said the landlord would lik
to have a word with me.

At first, I thought it was to tell me that the pony had passe
away. To my surprise he came and told me how honoured the
were to have us staying with them. He was a man who coul
remember the old coaching days, and the man in charge of th
stabling was an old groom who was quite excited at having som
horse flesh in his care again. He had given the pony a good brus
down and covered it with blankets and generally made it quite a
home. The landlord was thrilled by our proposed tour of th
Lakes, and insisted that we should spend the evening with him i
his private apartment, and there he introduced us to the importan
people of the district.

Next morning the pony certainly looked fitter than he had don
before, and most of the village turned out to give us a good send
off. I do not know what they had given the pony, but for the firs

me it shied. I had noticed traces of blood on its nostrils which iggested he had been eating corn all night. He trotted very riskly out of the village, but within two miles came to a full stop. here was no hill this time, and I could see no other reason except tree stump.

When I tried to get him to go forward he deliberately turned ound. I said to my wife: 'We have had enough to put up with rom him and I'm having no nonsense about this.' So I took the whip and sat up to drive past the stump at full speed. This time e could not stop, but swerved violently, and we found ourselves n the ditch on the opposite side of the road.

My wife, who by now was beginning to doubt my horseman-hip, decided to get out and walk, but in this respect she did not urn out to be as good a journeyman as the pony. I led him for a ittle way until he calmed down. As soon as he got the oats out of is system his spirit evaporated, and he became once more the bject animal he was before, and it was necessary to have long ests before we could complete our journey.

We eventually arrived at Grange-over-Sands, and it was with a reat sense of relief that we parked the pony with a nearby armer. We made up our minds that during the week we were taying there we would try to forget it.

Unfortunately, ponies are not like cars. They need constant ttention. Within two days the farmer came round to the hotel and sked how long we were staying. I said: 'A week'. He asked what ve were going to do about the pony. I asked him what he meant, nd he told me he only had one loose box and that the pony was icking the place down. The farmer also said he had nobody to xercise it. I certainly did not want to take him for a run with the rap, so my wife suggested taking it for a walk with us. I pointed out that this would limit our excursions to the main road, as it vould be rather difficult to get him over stiles. Fortunately we got a boy to ride him.

The fatal day came when we had to proceed on our journey. We vere going to Windermere to visit friends who were eagerly ooking forward to our arrival by this unusual form of transport.

It rained, and my wife conveniently found some friends who

were making the journey by car, so she decided to accompan them. She said she was beginning to appreciate what horsepowe meant in a car.

It was necessary to stud the pony every morning – that is, to pu nails in the shoes to prevent slipping. I remembered that by goin out of my way about four miles I could get to Cartmel, wher there was a blacksmith. The road to Cartmel is hilly, and as th horse was not properly shod I had to walk all the way in the rair I arrived at Cartmel only to find I was behind a queue. Apparentl everybody sent their horses to shoe on wet mornings. With view to enlisting the sympathy of the blacksmith, I went to th front and told him of my dilemma.

He came to have a look at my equipage, and then asked m whether by chance I was intending to sell the pony when I go home. I looked at him and a wild idea flashed through my mind. said: 'You have caught me in the right mood this morning. If yo are willing to treat lock, stock and barrel, I am prepared to sell ou now.' 'How much would you be wanting?' he asked. When said: 'I will tell you how much it cost – £150 in all', he replied: ' am only a poor lad, you know, I only have £120.' I tried to loo as if I was considering the matter. 'I am not in a position to giv you a written guarantee of his pedigree', I said at length, 'but can assure you he is not highly strung.'

When I accepted his offer, subject to the condition that he go me a conveyance to take me to Windermere, he dashed off on hi bicycle, leaving all his business, and came back with a taxi. H asked me if I was prepared to sign a declaration to justify the us of a taxi in wartime by stating I was on important business. Th bargain was struck.

My wife, when I arrived at Windermere, said with tears in he eyes that she didn't know how I could do such a thing. She onl hoped that the poor thing would have a good home. I console her by saying that the taxi-man had told me the blacksmith wa the best judge of horseflesh in the district. But considering th price of good horse meat during wartime, I was not sure whic way to take that.

18
CERTAIN VALUES

> Old age, believe me, is a good and pleasant time. It is true that you are gently shouldered off the stage, but then you are given such a comfortable front stall as spectator, and, if you have really played your part, you are more content to sit down and watch.
>
> JANE E. HARRISON

During the Second World War, I began to be worried as German bombs flattened Bradford Property Trust property in London and the major industrial towns. Until then I had never had a moment's financial anxiety. Discussing the problem with A.D. I said; 'Well Algy, it looks to me that we might lose the lot in this blitz business – perhaps we should try to find a way of spreading the risk.' It was suggested that Mr Fred Reddihough, the Yorkshire wool millionaire, might be willing to take an interest in the BPT and a meeting was arranged. He agreed to take a one third shareholding, for which he paid £130,000. This was the only capital introduced into the company since the original £1,000 at its inception.

This proved one of Mr Reddihough's most profitable investments. At the end of the war, property owners were surprised by the speed and fairness with which insurance claims were met. I believe only £200m was available against claims which would be in the region of £1,000m. We were greatly relieved when we heard that the Government accepted the full responsibility for this huge sum. Chiefly through the masterly handling of the situation by Sir Trestram Eve, the value for war damage was agreed while 'the tear was in the eye'. We had taken as little out of the business as we could, and as things became normal we quickly felt the benefit of our years of economy. We also shared in the benefit from inflated property and land values caused by scarcity conditions.

Soon after this I was surprised, when making one of my periodic surveys, to find that I had achieved on paper the target I had set myself when I started in business. Of course, thanks to inflation and taxation the amount was worth considerably less than it had been when I made it my target. I calculated that it was in fact worth about one half, and I adjusted my sights accordingly, though in doing so I tried to be careful not to forget the principle that had originally guided me – namely, to achieve what I had set out to do. Fortunately my family and I had not created an unduly high standard of living for ourselves. Our one extravagance was travel, and in our first trip abroad after the war we certainly let ourselves go by sending several food parcels home.

The day came when I added up my accounts again and found that, even taking my revised figure into consideration, I had achieved all that I had set myself. It was mostly on paper, which was not a marketable security, but I knew I should only be deluding myself if I did not acknowledge the truth. However, it was one thing to convince myself that I had reached my destination, and quite another to explain my position to my family, my friends and my business associates – as I soon discovered. For example, I was under a particular obligation to the last man who had put money into the business. In Yorkshire a man would not be expected to take a quixotic attitude to my withdrawal.

I went for a three-hour walk one Sunday morning and thought it all out. I decided there was only one thing to do. I would have to resign from the various companies with which I was associated. I came home, gathered the family together and explained the position. I was agreeably surprised that I was able to convince them I was doing the right thing. The only person who might easily suffer was my son. He had chosen my business because he liked my way of life and perhaps because he hoped to follow in my footsteps, but I was essentially a dealer who depended on intuition and long experience. If he had intuition he would not need me. If he had not, it was something I could not teach him. In any case I could not see any point in carrying on merely to amass wealth with its many obligations and few consolations. On the other hand, if I retired my son would be free to make his own life. He had acquired his professional qualifications as a surveyor and was assured of a good living. He could buy a professional practice or, if he preferred, go into property dealing on his own as I had done.

In any case, if I sold part of my interest in the company, I could make some provision for my family, which, provided I lived five years, would be free of death duties. On the other hand if I continued to acquire wealth on paper, my sudden death could mean that my son would have to keep his nose to the grindstone for many years to find the cash to pay them. Then, again, we are living in a rapidly changing world. It is far better to be equipped with an alert mind today than simply to have plenty of money.

I dropped the bombshell that same afternoon. I wrote to my colleague resigning my position as managing director in the various companies with which I was connected.

He was naturally very much concerned about this and at first could not understand my point of view. He thought it was a passing whim. He knew, too, that I was keen on having a farm of my own and suggested that I should arrange to have sufficient leisure to look after it. After several discussions he saw that I was adamant. He agreed with our other large shareholder to buy on generous terms from me what shares I wanted to realise. I was to have complete freedom, but would remain nominally managing director and responsible for the agricultural section of our business until a suitable man could be found to take my place.

It was all arranged in the long run; and although I have shed much of my responsibility, I still take a fatherly interest in this fascinating business, but mainly in an advisory capacity. Still, I am not so ambitious as the deacon of a chapel in Yorkshire, who, owing to the weight of his years, had been persuaded by the brethren to retire. He agreed, but asked if he might offer a prayer before relinquishing office. He said: 'Oh Lord if I can no longer be a labourer in your vineyard, will you use me in an advisory capacity?'

Although my interests are more varied I am still fully employed in the business of life, and I hope I always shall be. But I am spending less time in the market place, more under the cherry tree.

Like most things in life, expectation fails where most it promises. Now that I had gone into semi-retirement I had at last the chance to fulfil the one great ambition of my boyhood – to own a twelve-horse farm. The sizes of arable farms in our district were always reckoned by the number of horses kept. The smallest holding would have one horse. Father in his heyday had two horses, but no doubt he would have agreed with Thoreau that he was working more to keep the horse than the other way about. On any farm which had fewer than six horses or 200 acres the farmer himself would work.

My dream farm would have been just like the one where my father worked. It comprised about 400 acres. Of course, the real attraction for me was the gentleman's residence attached to the farm. As a boy I had occasional glimpses inside the house. Most of the rooms, including the nursery, had French windows on to the lawn. The furnishings, and particularly the library, remain in my mind as rich and colourful.

Apart from the aristocratic farmer and his wife there was a family of five or six young children of my generation, and I remember a ladylike governess. The red letter day in my life came when one of the girls invited me to play croquet on the lawn. There was also ample accommodation for guests. The kitchens and the dairy were spacious and always scrupulously clean. The domestic staff at that time consisted of three maids, and my mother would come in to help occasionally.

Also living in the servants' quarters were the single outdoor servants, the wagoner, the second and the groom. Outside were the vegetable gardens and the orchard. Besides the twelve shire horses the stables contained two hunters and a pony, which was not only ridden by the children but carried them about in their governess car. The grown-ups, of course, were in the dogcart. In the cottages nearby were the shepherd and gathman (or dairy-man) and five or six labourers. The blacksmith's shop was opposite the front gates.

The farmer's way of life appealed to my indolent nature because he spent his time supervising rather than using his hands. If not therwise engaged, he usually went round part of his farm every ıorning. He went to Sleaford market on Monday and Lincoln ıarket on Friday. There would also be plenty of days for hunting nd shooting during the winter season, and there would be tennis nd croquet parties during the summer.

It was not surprising, therefore, that each year as I grew older, vatching the corn ripen and the harvest being stacked, I had ostalgic longings to own a farm like this.

I knew that changes had taken place since my youth, but it was ot until I was in a position to buy a farm that I realised how little emained of the old way of life. Today it would need several housand acres to live up to the standard of my ideal farmer. For is type of farm, horses are now a luxury. Their work is largely one by machinery and mechanics have taken the place of the old arm labourer. The blacksmith's shop has been turned into an ngineering outfit and the domestic quarters into an accountant's ffice. Moreover, farming today is a business which requires a arge amount of capital, and is certainly not a novice's, much less a etired man's, job. Having been disillusioned about the notion of touring the countryside in a pony and trap and also about buying a farm, my wife and I decided to celebrate our semi-etirement by wintering in South Africa.

On the ship going out I met a young man who had been a arming pupil at the Manor House, Digby, my home village. He ıad emigrated to South Africa and had bought a sugar farm in Natal, to which he was returning. During the voyage he gave me a good insight into the growing of sugar cane. Soon after arriving n South Africa I met two Lincolnshire farmers who were ooking round for a sugar farm, and one of them planned to live n South Africa permanently to look after it. I mentioned to them hat if they came across anything bigger than they wanted I night be interested to go in with them. We kept in touch, and one day they came to me with an offer they had, to buy a 2,000 acre estate situated near the property of the man whom I had met on the ship.

On investigating the proposition I found the information I had received from him was most valuable. We decided to buy, but as we had only limited funds in South Africa we had to arrang a loan. We fixed an interview with a bank manager (who did no know us) in Durban. It was very hot, and my two friends turne up for the interview attired in shorts and shirt. This is the norm seaside dress in Durban, but one usually puts on a suit for mo formal business occasions. We told the manager we had come t borrow £60,000. He looked at my friends and said the accommo dation would have to be considered at board level, but he thougl that if the directors could have seen us personally they might hav lent us the money there and then at our face value. He asked us t return in forty-eight hours, which we did, to find the money wa at our disposal.

There was a fine residence on the estate with a swimming-poc and gardens with every kind of tropical fruit. Instead of the usu mud huts for natives which surrounded most sugar farms, ther was a compound containing concrete rooms to accommodate th 300 native boys who worked on the estate. A shop attached sol them everything they wanted. The natives were paid 3s a day for set piece of work (known as a 'task'). They were also given mealie and meat twice a week. At the time we were staying there, the started work about 4.30am, when a large bell was rung. The tas was done by piecework, which the boys usually finished by noor Our partner was a very progressive farmer, and by mechanisatio and the introduction of large quantities of manures he was able i less than three years to double the yield on the farm, and it is sti flourishing. At the end of this period, when he was in a positio to take over the farm, the other investor and myself made a amicable arrangement with him to be paid out. The whole of th venture had resulted from the coincidence of meeting a Digb man on the ship and seems to me a good example of giving luck chance.

A similar incident brought me good fortune in Australia. W had always wanted to visit that part of the world. In a train on day, after the Second World War, I met a man whom I knew to b the general manager of an insurance company. He was going t Australia in connection with his company's business. Knowin that they had first-class connections in Australia, I asked hin

n the spur of the moment if he would look out a good invest-
ient for me, and the next day I sent him a cheque for the amount
wished to invest. When he returned to this country, he said he
ad invested the money on the advice of their general manager
nd a firm of accountants, to whom he had given powers of
torney, subject to my approval.

This arrangement turned out successfully, and after two or three
ears I thought it would be worthwhile to visit Australia and
ieet the people who were looking after my business. I found that
irough judicious buying and selling on their part the capital had
.most doubled. Through the introduction of the insurance
ompany and the accountants, we were able to meet while we
ere there many of the important people in Australia, and in fact
e attended a small party at the home of Mr Menzies, the Prime
Iinister, on Old Year's Night, and had the pleasure of meeting
is charming family.

It was very hot and supper was served on the lawn. The haggis
as piped in, in true Scots fashion. With us that evening were
ir Don Bradman, whom we met on several subsequent occasions.
came to the conclusion that he was as adept at his business man's
esk as he was on the cricket pitch. Altogether we had a very
appy and successful trip to Australia – thanks to a chance
emark on a train.

The wide opportunities I had for travel came about because I
ad made my business impersonal. Had I been a professional man
would not have been so easy for me to leave my affairs. I have
ften noticed that people who build up a personal business find
iemselves tied to it, whereas it was necessary for me to employ
rofessional assistants and this gave me a certain amount of
eedom.

A colonel in the Engineers once startled me by saying that he
as unfortunate to be born with brains. He explained that this was
bserved at a very early age, and in consequence he passed all
is exams at school and in his profession. While his future was
lways assured, it meant that his life was mapped out in the
irection where his talents lay. In consequence, he had always
een doing work for people with more enterprise than himself

who had been using him in order to make money. This was mo
or less what I did. I found that my flair was only in the directic
of buying and selling, and it was necessary for me to find oth
people to do all the administrative work.

After the war, the main business of the company was centred i
London. Fred Bucke, who joined the company in 1930, starte
from scratch to build up a South London branch and eventual
became manager of the London branch and a director of th
company. When he retired he had a worthy successor in Fre
Boys, who also became a director of the company. It is now in th
capable hands of John Burgess, who is joint managing directo
with Jack Denham, who looks after the financial side of th
company's affairs.

When, at the beginning, A.D., a far-sighted man, said w
should have a pension scheme, I thought he was joking, as
the time we were fighting to survive on a year-to-year basis. No
I realise it was one of the best things that happened as most of th
staff remained with us until retiring age.

Algernon Denham died in 1961 and it was a great loss to th
Bradford Property Trust and a great loss to me personally, as w
had been close friends for forty years. He was engaged in busine
to the end, and actually took the chair at a board meeting a fe
days before he died.

On his death I reluctantly accepted the position of chairma
on a temporary basis. I was anxious we should carry through
public issue before the Capital Gains Tax came into force. Th
was fully underwritten but was not an immediate success, as
substantial sum was left with the underwriters. Probably th
combination of A.D.'s death and my age, which was the
seventy-two, may have led to the impression that I was pullin
out. However, this quickly righted itself.

Having launched the issue, the question arose of finding a ne
chairman. The obvious choice was Sir Henry Warner Bt. wh
was well known to Jack Denham, son of A.D. Sir Henry Warn
is chairman of Warner Estates Ltd, a public company founded b
his grandfather, Sir Courtenay Warner. The Warner Estate
properties and the management are similar to those of BPT.

He was approached with a view to his joining the board and ı due course taking my place as chairman. To this he agreed, roviding Warner Estates Ltd could acquire a substantial hareholding in the BPT from some of the existing shareholders. 'his was arranged.

Later still I retired altogether from active participation in the ompany's affairs. The board then invited me to become president nd I was glad to accept, not least because this left me in touch vith old friends and memories of 'battles long ago'.

The appointment of Sir Henry was indeed most fortunate, as ınder his leadership, the BPT has gone from strength to strength nd still retains the same basic principle. Safe as houses!

EPILOGUE

What delightful hosts are they –
  Life and love!
Lingeringly I turn away,
  This late hour, yet be glad enough
They have not witheld from me
Their high hospitality.
  So, with face lit with delight
And all gratitude, I stay
Yet to press their hands and say,
  'Thanks – so fine a time! Good night.'

JAMES WHITCOMBE RILEY

INDEX